Divorce in Peace
Alternatives to War from a Judge and Lawyer

Divorce in Peace

Alternatives to War from a Judge and Lawyer

JOHN AND LAURA
ROACH

Divorce in Peace: Alternatives to War from a Judge and Lawyer

Published by Wheatmark®
1760 East River Road, Suite 145
Tucson, Arizona 85718 USA
www.wheatmark.com

ISBN: 978-1-62787-372-7 (paperback)
ISBN: 978-1-62787-414-4 (hardcover)
ISBN: 978-1-62787-373-4 (ebook)
LCCN: 2015959241

We dedicate this book to our parents, and our boys: John, Jacob, and Jack. They inspire us to be better people, to maintain a sense of humor, challenge our ways of thinking, and let us know daily how truly blessed we are.

Contents

PART THREE
Negotiating the Issues

PART FOUR
Making It Legal

Appendices

Contents

About the Authors

John Roach is a Texas district court judge with a true passion for the law. Those who appear in his courtroom quickly learn he takes what he does and the decisions he has to make very seriously. As a judge, he has had a front row seat to over 10,000 family law cases. He has witnessed couples completely destroy their personal finances and family relationships in contested divorces. As a judge he also interviews children of those couples who are going through a divorce; he has had to listen to the heart wrenching stories these kids tell about the trouble in their home. John has watched as the adversarial nature of the Family Law court system has taken its toll on countless families. He knew there were better ways.

Laura Roach is best known for her high-energy personality and her uncanny ability to help people reach a resolution to their problems. As a Partner at the law firm of Albin Roach, a Family Law attorney and mediator she has helped over 2,000 families work through their divorce issues and has represented thousands of clients going through divorce. Like John, she has seen people who once loved each other turn against one another and fight until there is no fight left, and no money left to fight. As an attorney, she has been in the trenches fighting the battles that are required when people are forced to be adversaries in open court. As a mediator, she tries to salvage what is left after the case has gotten too far out of control. She also knew there were better ways.

John and Laura began a journey over eight years ago to pull the curtains back on the family law court system and expose the devastating approach most couples take when they divorce. They know neither the lawyers nor the clients are the problem. The problem lies in a system that sets up a husband and a wife as adversaries, two fighting forces where the supposed winner takes all. In reality, no one wins a war involving a family.

The experience John and Laura bring to the topic of divorce is immense. They have participated in each of the Alternative Dispute Resolution methods in this book. Throughout this book, John provides his insights in the Judge's Perspective and Laura in the Mediator's Perspective.

Introduction

Divorce is the legal dissolution of marriage. Few life events are as destructive and stressful, yet the divorce rate throughout the United States has remained high. Almost 50% of all marrying couples will divorce.

While the definition of divorce is simple enough, the exact path to divorce from beginning to end is difficult to predict. Through our experiences as legal professionals both as lawyers and judge for a combined 40 years, we have seen where divorcing couples go right and, more often, where they go wrong.

Couples who choose to divorce are quickly introduced to the Family Law court system. They are often ill-prepared and unrealistic about its purpose.

Many couples react to the word "divorce" by gearing up for a fight. One spouse calls a friend who went through a nasty divorce and asks for a referral to the most hard-hitting attorney in town. The other spouse, likewise, finds the meanest divorce lawyer he or she can find. When preparing for war, it's natural to line up a great offense. For a family, however, war is hell.

Our mission is to revolutionize the way couples approach divorce by informing, educating, and empowering them to take control of their circumstances and resolve their disputes with minimal damage to themselves, their kids, and their finances.

In this book, we will show you:

- How the family law court system works.
- The high costs of fighting over a divorce.
- Peaceful methods for settling a divorce without a court trial.
- Practical solutions for resolving the issues surrounding a divorce.
- The legal steps required to make your divorce official.

In addition to learning the lessons and information in this book, we think it is crucial for couples who want to Divorce in Peace to find like-minded professionals—attorneys, financial planners, mental health professionals and others—who are committed to the same principles of peaceful resolution. These professionals are listed at our website, www.divorcein-peace.com. Each of the attorneys have committed to the *Divorce in Peace Pledge* found at Appendix A.

A word of caution: If there are issues involving family violence or physical abuse to you or your children, then you might be better served by hiring a lawyer and getting immediate protection from the courts. This book will certainly help you understand the issues you will need to address, but trying to cooperate with or settle a matter with a person who engages in such behavior is neither helpful nor healthy.

We have been involved in well over 20,000 Family Law

cases. An overwhelming number of them are settled out of court using the various Alternative Dispute Resolution, ADR, methods we will discuss. The reason we decided to write this book is the number of cases we have witnessed going to trial; we have had a front-row seat to the destruction of families, both emotionally and financially.

It is hard to imagine how two people who once loved each other can now make it their mission to destroy each other. Ironically, this mission ultimately results in destroying themselves in the process.

Most couples, however, can successfully settle their divorce outside of the courts. Whatever your situation, *Divorce in Peace* will help you identify your options, study the alternatives, and create a plan.

In short, we hope to help you avoid the often expensive, emotional, public, and destructive parts of our family court system. Divorce is never pleasant, but with the right knowledge and tools, it can be peaceful. You, your spouse, and your kids deserve peace.

Part One

WAR OR PEACE?

1

Do We Really Want a Divorce?

The worst reconciliation is better than the best
divorce.

Miguel de Cervantes Saavedra

The only sure-fire way to avoid an all-out divorce war is to not
get a divorce. In the practice of law we have found couples
often throw out the "D" word in anger, or they are at the
end of their rope and want to get their spouse's attention. But
when all is said and done, is divorce the right course of action?

If you are considering divorce, first make certain you have
done all you can to keep your marriage together. For those who
are thinking about divorce because of financial, emotional, or
communication problems, take a deep breath and think about
what you can actually accomplish with divorce. The issues that
will arise during the divorce process will put an even greater
strain on your finances, emotions, and your ability to communicate. Lastly, if you have kids, you at least owe them the con-
certed effort to do all you can before going the divorce route.

Financial Issues

If you are having financial problems, join the crowd. Overall consumer debt is at an all-time high, while overall savings is at an all-time low. If your personal finances are following this trend, this combination can have a devastating effect on your family's ability to meet its obligations, increasing stress on you and your marriage. In fact, almost 80% of young couples who divorce by the age of 30 report their financial problems were the primary cause of their divorce.

A simple answer to your financial problems might be helped by examining where your money is going. A financial planner will tell you that financial problems are not the result of how little money you earn, but rather how much money you spend. How much money do you spend? If you are like most couples, you have no idea.

Financial computer software like Quicken or Microsoft Money Plus, or a good app, makes it easy to track expenses. These programs/apps are simple to set up on your computer or smart phone and are made for those who aren't computer gurus. These programs/apps also allow you to upload your banking records (including account balances, deposits, debit card transactions, etc.) and other financial account information to help better track your expenses. Once you enter the information, use the software/app's tools to graphically display where your money is going. You will be amazed to learn where you spend your money. After you track where your money is going, you can see where some expenses could be cut and set monthly budgets for you and your spouse— and often times, your kids.

In addition to financial software, you might also find some help reading books on financial planning for couples.

We recommend several books: *Your Money or Your Life* by Joe Dominguez and Vicki Robin, *The Millionaire Next Door* by Thomas Stanley and William Dunko, and *The Family CFO* by Mary Claire Allvine. These books are great books for you to explore the value you place on money, how to set out and achieve financial goals and how to get out of debt.

Other books worth reading are *Talking Money: Everything You Need to Know about Your Finances and Your Future* by Jean Chatzky and *Conscious Spending for Couples: Seven Skills for Financial Harmony* by Deborah Knuckey. Another very helpful book is *Personal Finance for Dummies* by Eric Tyson.

Some great apps dealing with financial planning that are available for smart phones are: HomeBudget with Sync, Dollarbird, Moneywiz, Level Money and Mint.com.

If you just cannot get a handle on your finances through computer software, apps or books, you may benefit from the advice of a financial planner. Financial planners can assist you in developing strategies to monitor your cash flow, prioritize your debts, and how to more appropriately monitor your spending. They will take a look at your short- and long-term financial goals and explore various money management techniques to maximize your current assets against your debt.

For example, does taking out a home equity loan to pay off credit card debt make sense based upon your current financial situation? Which bills should be paid off first? Should you get a debt consolidation loan? A comprehensive financial plan will include an in-depth evaluation with you and your spouse about your personal goals and your goals as a couple. You can also expect a good financial planner to insist on thoroughly analyzing your and your spouse's spending and earnings and, if need be, recommend how to tighten your belt.

We have a list of financial planners in your area at www. divorceinpeace.com who understand how financial difficulties can put stress on a marriage as well as the stress of a possible divorce. Each of them have pledged to the principles of Divorce in Peace. See if they can help.

In addition to computer programs, apps, self-help books, and financial planners, there are many well-known, reputable non-profit credit counseling agencies that can assist you in making payment arrangements with creditors, including credit card companies. Be warned and pick your credit counseling agency carefully! Do your research; check their references and your local Better Business Bureau and the impact of using a credit counseling agency might have on your credit score.

Finally, if you and your spouse cannot find relief or satisfaction with a financial planner or credit counseling agency, you may want to explore personal bankruptcy. While drastic, bankruptcy is often a necessary step in getting your finances on the right footing. Consult a bankruptcy attorney to determine if you qualify for bankruptcy and whether it can actually meet your expectations.

Marriage Counseling

Have both of you tried marriage counseling? When asked why they are getting divorced, more often than not couples explain a difficulty in communicating with their spouse, a horrible argument over money, an annoying habit of their spouse, or an extra-marital affair. These themes seem to pervade most marriages in some form or another.

Once you see it often enough you begin to realize no one is without faults. Snoring, angry outbursts, lack of affection, gambling, spending too much money, not helping with the kids, shopping sprees—and the list goes on and on! What folks

Financial Resources

Financial PC Software

- Quicken (www.quicken.intuit.com)
- Microsoft Money (www.microsoft.com/money)
- You Need a Budget Pro (www.youneedabudget. com)
- Mint.com (free online personal finance software)

Books

- Your Money or Your Life by Joe Dominguez and Vicki Robin
- The Millionaire Next Door by Thomas Stanley and William Dunko
- The Family CFO by Mary Claire Allvine
- Talking Money: Everything Your Need to Know about Your Finances and Your Future by Jean Chatzky
- Conscious Spending for Couples: Seven Skills for Financial Harmony by Deborah Knuckey
- Personal Finance for Dummies by Eric Tyson

(continued)

Apps

- Home Budget with Sync, $4.99
- Dollarbird, $1.99
- Moneywix, $4.99
- Level Money, Free
- Mint.com, Free

Websites for finding financial planners

- www.divorceinpeace.com
- www.fpaforfinancialplanning.org (Financial Planning Association website, relevant articles and advice on financial planners)
- www.cfp.net (website for Certified Financial Planner Board of Standards, Inc.)
- http://www.sec.gov/answers/finplan.htm (SEC advice on financial planners)

---

don't realize is that the next person they meet and care about will have other annoying habits and propensities which, over time, become as problematic and frustrating as their spouse's. Our website at www.divorceinpeace.com has a list of marriage counselors who have committed to the *Divorce in Peace* principles and who know that the best way to avoid war is not to get a divorce, but if divorce is the only option, do it peacefully.

Like the options available for personal finances, there are a myriad of options for couples seeking outside help and guidance for their marriage. There are thousands of books on marriage—some with an emphasis on marriages with children—others without. Some focus on the religious aspects of conflict in marriage, while others deal with the differences between men and women. Whichever self-help book you choose, be sure it addresses your and your spouse's specific struggles and goals in the marriage.

One book we have enjoyed reading and have recommended to others is *His Needs, Her Needs* by William Harley. This book, as well as a weekend seminar, helps couples find out about the needs of their spouse, which are more than likely different from the other's needs. Once the needs have been identified, the book sets out a comprehensive plan on how to meet those needs of the other. When your spouse is happy, you are happy and vice versa. This book, as well as Harley's other books, is straightforward and leaves out the psychological mumbo-jumbo often seen in other books of this type.

Addiction Counseling and Treatment

Ten percent of any population is addicted to drugs or alcohol. We usually associate addiction with drugs and alcohol, but there are others: gambling, food, internet, video games and work. Addiction is defined as the strong and harmful need to regularly have something (such as a drug) or do something (such as gamble). To the spouse of an addict, addiction is the root of all problems. It diminishes, damages and endangers the family. The spouse having to deal with addiction has been lied to, cheated on, manipulated and minimized. The focus of the family was how to avoid conflict with the addict. The focus of the mom or dad has been on protecting the kids.

If you do not have any kids with the addict, you have many more choices than those who do. For those who have kids, the addict is still the mother or father of your child. You will have to have a relationship with that person for a long time, or at least until the child becomes an adult. In light of the past, you will have to decide if giving him or her another chance is worth the investment of time, money and emotions.

You are probably sick of hearing it, but addiction is a disease. It certainly does not excuse the behavior that you have had to endure, but it does provide you with some context into the behavior. The addict will never be cured of his or her disease. However, it can be managed effectively given the right tools, including treatment by professionals.

The first and foremost consideration is your safety and the safety of your kids. If you can confirm you are safe and that your kids are safe, then you can begin to explore treatment options. You can find addiction counselors and treatment centers at www.divorceinpeace.com, search the internet or ask friends for recommendations.

For the addict, if you want your marriage to work and/or you want an ongoing relationship with your children, you can no longer be in denial and you must get professional help. Too many addicts want to work on their relationship with their spouse and kids while in the initial stage of treatment. You must concentrate on yourself first! Once the disease is being treated, only then can you begin to repair the damaged relationships around you.

Counseling for the Children

You and your spouse may have tried all the counseling you care to. You might think counseling didn't help or it wasn't worth the cost. But what about your children? Have both of you considered counseling for them? If you think your kids haven't noticed and haven't been affected by your less-than-perfect marriage, you are dead wrong. Look for a counselor who has extensive training and experience in helping children. Your children need someone they can speak with openly. If divorce is the ultimate outcome, they will need even more attention. Why do Mom and Dad have separate homes? Did I do something to cause them to split up? Is this all my fault? These questions will come up no matter the child's age. You cannot handle your own emotions and your children's at the same time. Leave it to the professionals. A list of child counselors in your area is also available at www.divorceinpeace. com.

Divorce Counseling

Even if you don't go through marriage counseling, you may want to explore divorce counseling and/or co-parenting counseling or classes. What's the difference? Marriage counseling's goal is to help couples work together through issues in hope of bettering an ongoing relationship. Divorce counseling and co-parenting classes are designed to assist couples with the issues that will arise during and after divorce. How do you handle the kids living in two homes? What are the ground rules on attending extracurricular activities? How are you going to handle introducing the children to your or your spouse's new boyfriend or girlfriend?

While some of these situations are currently unimaginable, they will occur. Having a neutral person there to assist you through these issues will help you and, as a result, help your children.

Mediator's Perspective
Is Divorce the Answer?

As a mediator, I see couples who are at the end of their rope and just want to be divorced, now. I always ask, "Why are you getting divorced?" Sometimes I hear tragic stories of emotional and physical abuse, a husband or wife who is a perpetual cheater, liar or drug user, and the list goes on. However, a lot of the time I hear, "We grew apart", "He never helps me with the kids" or "We really don't have anything in common anymore."

I always follow up with, "What have you done to save your marriage?"

What I am about to say does not apply to cases of physical or emotional abuse, perpetual cheating, drug users or severe mental illness. If these are facts in your case, you may have no other choice but to move on. What I am about to say does apply to everyone else.

Marriage is tough. I have rarely met a couple who, at one time or another, had not at least given some thought about divorce. It is not healthy, but it is natural. We all possess a natural instinct when faced with an impossible situation to either fight or flight. Do I have what it takes within me to fight? Or am I too exhausted to fight anymore?

About 12 years ago I mediated a case of a couple who had been married for six years and had twin daughters who were two years old. When they came to my office, their final trial was scheduled in a month. Each had spent roughly $25,000 on attorney's fees. They only came to Mediation because the court ordered them to go prior to trial.

(continued)

The husband had cheated on his wife and he did not want to reconcile. The wife was willing to forgive him and wanted to remain married. When I asked the husband why he wanted a divorce he complained about what most people would complain about when they have two - 2 year olds at home—being tired, frustrated, ignored, no time alone and a loss of connection and affection with his wife. Having toddlers is a rough time.

In talking with them I could sense that they were not certain they wanted a divorce. At other times it seemed like they were dead set on getting a divorce. So I went forward with the mediation in an attempt to resolve all the divorce issues, but something kept nagging at me. Maybe there was something in their relationship that could be salvaged.

At the end of the day I had worked out a settlement for their divorce. Unbeknownst to the couple, I also put together another plan for them to reconcile if that was still an option. As we approached decision time in the mediation, the couple decided to try the reconciliation plan.

All this couple needed was a plan to move forward with their damaged relationship. They were on the verge of divorce, but wanted to give their relationship one more try. They were able to find something in the mediation that had not been there in a while—communication. In fact, this couple is still married today.

I am not saying that every couple who wants a divorce should or is going to reconcile. All I suggest is for you to make sure that divorce is the right option for you right now. If it is not, then keep trying. If it is, please Divorce in Peace.

Summing Up

Marriage is tough. Divorce is tougher. We don't intend for you to stay in a destructive, abusive relationship. If you are, however, one of the many couples we have met that have problems with communication, affection, respect, and money, you are not alone. Every relationship has problems. Most of the problems can be solved with the right tools and a lot of hard work. If you think there is a possibility of staying together, you at least need to explore the option of getting help. There is an extensive network of professionals who can help you through your marital problems. When all is said and done, you want to look back on your life and marriage and make sure you did everything you possibly could to preserve the relationship.

If you have children, you owe it to them to make sure you are making the right decision in divorcing their other parent. The decision you make will impact them as well.

If you are at the point that you have tried as hard as you can, explored every opportunity to make the relationship work, and are just ready to move on, we understand. All we ask is that you learn everything you can about the divorce process and do everything you can to Divorce in Peace. Read on and learn about the alternatives available to help you get through the divorce in a way that minimize self-destruction and financial ruin.

2

Two Ways to Get a Divorce

What lies behind us and what lies before us are
tiny matters compared to what lies within us.

Unknown

There are two general ways to get a divorce:
- Fight it out in the court system, or
- Settle your disagreements outside of court.

It's your choice.

Going to War: Ready, Aim, Fire

Let's say you decide to go the more traditional, high-conflict approach. You will probably start by telling your friends
that you're thinking about divorcing your spouse. In an effort
to gain a perceived advantage, you let them know all the dirt
that has been going on in your home. In support of you, they
are aghast at what you have been going through. They recommend the meanest divorce lawyer they know.

Next, you start gathering all of the bad stuff you have against your spouse, from emails to texts to pictures to calendars and diaries. You then head to your lawyer's office prepared for war. You meet with the attorney. During your consultation, you tell your attorney about your assets and your position regarding child custody.

Regarding property, the attorney will likely advise you to go home and try to gain access into the family computer containing all the financial records. If you don't know how to do this, the attorney can send over a computer analyst to download all the information on the hard drive for later inspection. Also, you'll be advised to gather all the financial documents you can and, perhaps, remove money from bank accounts before filing for divorce. Start gathering up the credit card and debit card statements. Turn over greeting cards and other letters your spouse has sent or written to you over the years of the marriage. Write down all the other nasty things about your spouse you can think of—just in case you missed something earlier.

On the child custody issues, the lawyer will likely advise you to start a calendar detailing your and your spouse's daily contact with kids. Include the duties and responsibilities each of you undertake for the kids: who gets them up in the morning, who feeds them breakfast, takes them to school, picks them up, does homework, takes them to the doctor, who puts them to bed. Start gathering pictures of you and your kids to show the judge. If legal in your state, start privately recording your conversations with your spouse or, better yet, arguments you and your spouse are having about the kids. Gather as much information you have on your involvement with the kids as possible. Once you gather all the information, head back to the attorney's office, proud of your accomplishments.

All of the information acquired will be used in open court to prove you should win! And remember that while you're busy doing this, another lawyer is probably having your spouse do the very same thing to show the judge why your spouse should win.

Oh, one more thing. To complete the hiring process, the attorney will ask you for money—an advance payment called a Retainer. Unlike any other business, the lawyer knows all of the assets you have before she tells you how much you will be charged. A marital estate worth $100,000 may be quoted a $2,500 retainer, while an estate reaching $750,000 could be quoted a $20,000 retainer, or more.

After gathering all the needed information, your attorney is ready to file for divorce. You will now have to help the attorney decide on where the divorce papers should be served: at home, the office, baseball practice? So many choices. The battle lines are drawn.

Many folks will read this and fault the lawyer in setting up a case like this, but that's unfair. It's the lawyer's job to do this. They are merely operating within the adversarial system of family law.

Finally, after a year of legal wrangling and paying huge amounts in attorney's fees, your divorce case goes to trial. The lawyers present all the evidence collected, each trying to prove that the other spouse is at fault and their client should get more of everything. A myriad issues are laid on the table: Who gets the house? Where will the kids live? How often will each parent get to see them? What about the 401K? The list goes on and on.

Who makes all these decisions? A judge—someone you have never met. Odds are, you will not like what the judge decides.

The court system is adversarial by nature, it takes fire to fight fire. You have to decide if this is the way you want to go.

Judge's Perspective
Gambling Away Your Money and Your Kids

Would you go to Vegas and bet your life savings on a spin of the roulette wheel? How about playing high-stakes poker using your kids as the chips? Although people argue that gambling for entertainment is okay, gambling your life savings or your kids' future is not okay—in fact, it's stupid.

Going to court is like going to Vegas. While attorneys can certainly advise you on your odds of winning, no one can predict how your case will ultimately be decided. True, the judge has to follow the law, but no law tells a judge exactly what to do in your case. Instead, they use phrases such as "fair and equitable" and "in the child's best interest," which are open to interpretation. The judge is human and makes decisions based on certain beliefs about what is best.

Think about it. Suppose you and your spouse cannot agree on how to split the $100,000 that you have accumulated during your marriage. You each spend $10,000 on attorneys to try to win in court. Now the fight is over the remaining $80,000. So you take your dispute to the casino (the court). You go to the roulette table and put your $40,000 on red, and your spouse puts $40,000 on black.

(continued)

You spin the wheel (present your case to the judge) and hold your breath, hoping for a positive outcome. On the roulette table, you may win or lose. In court you can win, lose some of your bet, or lose it all.

When you are dealing with your kids, you put even more on the table. You bet on which parent your children will live with, how much time you will get to spend with them, where they will go to school, what medical care they will receive, and anything else you and the other parent cannot agree to. Then you spin the wheel and see what your relationship with your children will look like. Again, it sounds so absurd.

Truthfully, judges try their hardest to do the right thing for families. However, what the judge thinks is fair and equitable or in your children's best interest probably does not match what you think. Once the judge makes a decision, it's over. As soon as you loaded up your casino chips and walked into the courtroom, you lost control.

Do not gamble with your hard-earned money. Do not gamble with the relationship you have with your kids. Stay out of the casino. The two people who are in the best position to make these decisions are you and your spouse. Keep control and stay out of court.

Choosing Peace

This book sets out specific, proven methods on how to resolve your divorce short of all-out war. These methods are called Alternative Dispute Resolution (ADR). The premise of

ADR is spouses can work together to settle the issues involved in their divorce. It puts control in the hands of the couple, not the court.

Instead of running to the computer to download every piece of financial information gathered during the marriage, go to the computer together and look at information collectively in a manner where each of you can be satisfied. Make a copy of the hard drive so that each of you will have access to its contents. This way you will both have the financial information you need to adequately address how to solve the financial issues that will arise as a result of divorce.

Instead of listing your child's activities to prove your spouse doesn't participate in them enough, review the activity schedule to see how you both can maximize your time with your child. Focus on your child's future and relationship with each of you, rather than digging up the past in an effort to curtail the child's contact with the other parent.

Instead of paying your lawyer to prove that your spouse is a horrible person who doesn't deserve your money or your kids, sit down with your spouse and listen respectfully to each other's desires and concerns. Instead of going to court and letting a judge make all the decisions, negotiate with your spouse to find solutions that you both agree with. Your efforts will result in a divorce settlement that is tailored to your situation, needs, and desires—as it should be.

Summing Up

War or peace? Those are the two ways to get a divorce. In war, the gloves are off and the fighting goes on until the final bell, when the judge makes the decision. In peace, the couple maintains control of the outcome and significantly decreases the amount of stress, money, and time spent on the divorce.

This chapter has given you just a taste of how the ADR process works. In the next chapter, you'll learn more about the differences between ADR and getting a divorce in court. Later chapters explain the different ADR methods and how to use them to negotiate the issues in your divorce. For now, the most important point to understand is that divorce does not have to be a battle.

You can choose the peaceful way.

3

The Family Court System

A lawyer is never entirely comfortable with a friendly divorce, any more than a good mortician wants to finish his job and then have the patient sit up on the table.

Jean Kerr

Some of you still might not be convinced that your divorce issues can be resolved in a peaceful way. This chapter will take you step-by-step through what a divorce in court looks like.

Getting a divorce through the court system is not a simple process. It is governed by specific procedural and substantive rules. These rules hinder those who are not familiar with them and aid those who have mastered them.

Nor is going to court a private matter. The courts are a public forum, which means they are open to anyone who wants to watch. The documents filed with the court are available to anyone who wants to see them.

The family court system was designed to be adversarial, pitting one spouse against the other. One spouse files a lawsuit for divorce. The other spouse answers the lawsuit. If you cannot reach an agreement, you go to court. Each side presents evidence to a neutral third party (the judge and, in some states, a jury), and the judge decides who gets which assets, how much time you get to spend with your kids and all other issues you and your spouse can't agree on.

We don't want you to go through an adversarial process, but we think it's important to show you how the court system works for two reasons. First, we want you to know exactly what you can avoid by divorcing in peace. Second, even if you choose to Divorce in Peace, you can't avoid the court system entirely. You will still need to file divorce paperwork with a court and have the court finalize your divorce. The difference is what happens in-between. As we explain the steps in getting a divorce through the court system, we will also point out how the process differs if you are divorcing in peace. Appendix H provides a flow chart of the Family Law Court System.

Filing for Divorce

Whether you are settling your divorce in court or through ADR, the first step is the same. To begin the divorce process, you or your spouse must file divorce paperwork in a court in the county in which you live. In legal terms, one of you has to file a lawsuit for divorce. This original paperwork is called a Petition or Complaint, depending on your state. The spouse who files for divorce is called the Petitioner (or Plaintiff). The other spouse is called the Respondent (or Defendant).

All states have some sort of residency requirement before filing for divorce. Some states require that you have resided in the state for six months and in the county for three months. Other states require a lesser period of residency, while still others require only that you are a resident of the state on the date you file the Petition or Complaint.

The Petition or Complaint filed with the court is very specific and will differ from state to state. While you can find very generic divorce forms on line, you would be better served to find forms specifically for your state, or hire an attorney.

There are many books and online companies who sell "Do-It-Yourself" divorce kits where you can file and complete your own divorce. Also, many counties in many states have law libraries where they provide packets of forms (usually for a nominal charge) you will need to file and finalize your divorce. Check with your local law library to find out if they provide this service. Some states have set up websites that provide divorce papers and instructions for free. Check in your state and see what resources are available for you, or you can go to Helpful Links at www.divorceinpeace.com. You can also consult with an attorney who will be able to file your divorce for you.

Some states require a separation period prior to filing the divorce paperwork. Once any such separation period has passed and you have completely filled out the forms, you are ready to file. Head to your courthouse and file the paperwork with the court clerk. You will be required to pay a filing fee, unless you can provide adequate proof that you are indigent.

Keep in mind that some states have waiting periods for divorce. In those states, you must wait for a certain period of time between the time the divorce papers are filed and the time the divorce can be finalized.

The ADR Approach

Upon filing the Petition for Divorce, it is time to begin in earnest to resolve the issues surrounding your divorce. Whichever ADR process you choose will usually begin at this point.

Service

Every lawsuit, including a divorce, requires the person being sued (the Respondent) to be notified of the suit by being given a copy of the Petition or Complaint. This notification is called Service.

Service can be accomplished in several ways. The more adversarial method is for a local constable or a private authorized person (a Process Server) to serve the lawsuit on the respondent. It is very much like in the movies, when someone appears out of the blue, hands the person papers from the court, and says, "You have been served". While certainly not as dramatic as it plays out on television, being served in this way can be quite embarrassing and can set a negative tone for the remainder of the divorce. Many people don't ever get over the embarrassment of being served in front of their children, families, or co-workers.

An alternative method is a Waiver of Service. The waiver is a document signed by the Respondent acknowledging that the Respondent has received a copy of the Petition or Complaint. Some waivers also include language stating that the signer does not require additional notification of any hearings or the final trial. It is not advisable to sign such a broad waiver. We would lean toward a more limited waiver of service that simply says the divorce paperwork has been received.

The ADR Approach

If your goal is to Divorce in Peace, the Waiver of Service is the recommended process. Decide which of you is going to file for divorce. The other spouse will sign the Waiver of Service.

If you are served with a Petition for Divorce and are not filing a Waiver of Service, you have a limited time to send an answer to the court. The answer is an acknowledgement to the court that you have received a copy of the Petition for Divorce and know the divorce has been filed. Read your paperwork thoroughly to determine the time frame you have to respond. Once you respond, the court is aware that everyone who needs to be notified of the suit has been notified.

Temporary Restraining Orders and Standing Orders

Just saying the words "temporary restraining order" upsets many people, because they associate this term with family violence. However, a Temporary Restraining Order (TRO) is not the same thing as a protective order.

Have you ever heard about a case where someone who has just been served with a Petition for Divorce runs to the bank and takes all the money, then cancels the spouse's cell phone and charge cards? It does happen. So the law in each state allows people filing for divorce to ask the court to issue an order to prevent harmful things like these from happening. A

TRO prohibits actions such as cancelling accounts, removing money, damaging real or personal property, visiting or calling the spouse's place of employment, harassing the spouse or the spouse's family, and committing family violence. The violation of the TRO can result in a finding of contempt, which is punishable by a fine, confinement in jail and/or the payment of your spouse's attorney's fees.

Depending on the state, the TRO usually expires after a short period of time because it's issued after reviewing evidence from only one of the spouses. This is contrary to our generalized understanding of how the judicial process works. Therefore, another hearing is set for a short time later so the other spouse can tell his or her side of the story.

Temporary restraining orders are becoming standard practice for divorce. Because almost every case requires a TRO and a quick hearing, TROs have become burdensome to the family court system. For this reason, many counties have begun to impose Standing Orders that automatically apply whenever a divorce is filed. These orders have the same force and effect as a TRO, so there is no need to request one. The violation of a Standing Order is also punishable by contempt.

The ADR Approach

If you're attempting to resolve your issues amicably and standing orders aren't in place, you probably don't need a TRO. Instead, you and your spouse can agree in writing that neither of you will do anything to damage, hide, or otherwise dispose of property, cancel credit cards or bank accounts, show up at each other's place of employment, keep the children from the other parent, or withdraw the children from school.

Temporary Orders

Settling a divorce can take many months. Divorcing couples need ground rules for what will happen during that time: who is going to live in the house, who is responsible for paying what bills, where paychecks will be deposited, where the kids are going to live, how often each spouse can be with the children, and so on. When the divorce goes through the court system, these questions are decided by a judge. The judge holds a hearing and issues temporary orders that define the ground rules.

Temporary orders are just that—temporary. They are binding only while the case is pending, from the time the divorce is filed until it is final. They do not dictate the terms of the final settlement.

The ADR Approach

Instead of getting temporary orders from a judge, you and your spouse can work together to reach a temporary agreement about how to handle the immediate issues. You can reach that agreement using any of the ADR methods set out in this book.

However you get there, having temporary orders or a temporary agreement can allow you and your spouse to take a deep breath and see how things play out. If necessary, the temporary orders or agreement can be changed before the divorce becomes final.

Discovery

The Discovery Process (investigation/learning phase) provides each side the opportunity to learn as much about the information the opposing side has in their possession. It is also used to help determine the assets and liabilities of the marriage and, if kids are involved, find out information about child custody and visitation issues.

If the case proceeds to trial, Discovery can be the most expensive part of a case. Discovery includes: request for important, relevant documents (production of documents), written questions to the other spouse who must answer them under oath (interrogatories), request for records from other sources like schools or banks (subpoenas), request of the other spouse to admit certain facts (request for admissions), and request for the other side or other people to be questioned under oath (depositions).

Discovery is an opportunity for the spouses (also known as "parties") of the divorce to request, receive, examine, and use various types of information to prove their theory of the case or defeat the other's. In the context of litigation, the information will be used in court to convince the judge to see it their way or to disprove allegations made by the other spouse.

The ADR Approach

Discovery is less formal, but still important. You and your spouse will gather the information needed to resolve the issues around your divorce. Once the information has been gathered to your satisfaction, both of you will be able to fully examine it.

When dealing with the financial issues surrounding a divorce—the equitable division of the assets and debts acquired during the marriage—one of the most important discovery tools is the Inventory and Appraisement (I&A).

An I&A is a detailed and thorough disclosure of all of the assets and liabilities of each spouse and whether it is characterized as community/marital property (generally debts and assets acquired during the marriage) or separate property (generally property acquired before the marriage). The I&A is "sworn to," meaning it is signed in the presence of a notary, the effect of which is the person submitting the document is swearing under oath that it is true and correct to the best of his or her knowledge under the penalty of perjury.

Whether you resolve your divorce issues through ADR or litigation, both spouses will need to provide the other spouse a sworn (under oath) I&A.

Child Custody Evaluations

In some litigated cases, the court may order, or the spouses may agree to hire, a qualified individual to prepare a child custody evaluation to be filed with the court. A Child Custody Evaluation is usually prepared by a licensed professional counselor, or equivalent, who interviews the spouses, child and others who may live in the homes where the child lives or visits. The evaluator may also inspect the living conditions of each spouse, visit the school where the child is enrolled and speak with references provided by the parents. Finally, they sometimes perform psychological evaluations of the parties and/or the child. With all the information they have gathered they will prepare a final report for the court and will often make recommendations to the court regarding which parent the child should primarily live with, the time the child should spend with the other parent and other recommendations the evaluator believes are in the best interest of the child.

Remember in litigated cases these reports are provided to the court (the judge) to review, meaning they can be public records viewable at the courthouse by anyone unless specifically sealed by the court. Most importantly, while the evaluator makes recommendations to the court it is completely within the court's discretion to adopt the recommendations, adopt some of the recommendations or ignore the recommendations completely. A full Child Custody Evaluation can cost upwards of $20,000 and is merely a recommendation.

The ADR Approach

Usually a Child Custody Evaluation is not needed when parents are using an ADR method. However, if the parents cannot agree on child issues in ADR, they can have a Child Custody Evaluation conducted to provide information from which negotiations could begin and would not be provided to the court.

Mediation

If you are headed to court to have the judge make the decisions about your property and children, it is highly likely you will be ordered by the court to attend Mediation. Mediation is a process in which a neutral third party tries to help you reach an agreement. While this process can be helpful, court-ordered mediation often doesn't occur until shortly before the trial. By then you will have spent the majority of your money on attorney's fees, and the animosity between you and your spouse may have risen to a level that is beyond repair.

The ADR Approach

To Divorce in Peace—and reduce costs—use Mediation or another ADR process at the beginning of the divorce process, not the end. Mediation is discussed in Chapter 7.

Trial

If you are in a litigated divorce, and you have not arrived at an agreement through an ADR method, the final stage is the trial. Trial is your day in court. On this day your lawyer will stand up and make an opening statement, call witnesses on your behalf, cross examine individuals your spouse calls as witnesses, introduce documentary evidence, and then wrap it up in a closing argument in a last attempt to persuade the judge to find your way.

In the end, the judge will listen to all the evidence and make a decision on an equitable division of your property, which can include an order for the sale of certain property and to divest your interest in others. The judge will also decide what is in your children's best interest: where they will primarily live, how often the other parent will get to see them, where they will go to school, and any other issue on which you and your spouse have been unable to agree. All of these decisions will be included in a Final Decree/Order that the judge will sign.

The ADR Approach

Using ADR lets you avoid the trial. Instead of battling each other in court, you and your spouse resolve your issues outside of court, perhaps with assistance from a mediator, attorneys, or an arbitrator. You will then be ready to put your agreements in writing and file them with the court.

How Long Does a Court Divorce Take?

The invention of ADR processes had as much to do with the overcrowding of the family law court system as it did with resolving disputes amicably. A litigated divorce can take from six months to years to complete, depending on many factors. These factors include the case load of the courts in a particular county and how many times couples have to go to court to get matters resolved. If one or both spouses try to use the court to punish their spouse or run to court for every small issue, the case can drag out for years.

The frustrating part of the court system is often the number of times you have to appear to get an issue heard and, once at the courthouse, how long it takes the judge to call your case. Many times you can show up on a Monday and are told to come back later in the week or, in the worst case, be told to return months later. The cost of an attorney preparing for the same hearing multiple times is enormous. If the parties argue every little thing, the number of visits to the courthouse increase and the cost of litigation increases exponentially.

Judge's Perspective
If You Go to Court, Lower Your Expectations

When I first became a judge, I figured that half the people who came before me would not be happy with my decisions. What I soon realized is that *more* than half of the people who leave my courtroom every day are unhappy with the result of their case. More times than not, everyone is unhappy.

It is human for each of us to look at facts and circumstances in a light most favorable to ourselves. This happens in court as well. People think "If the judge could only see it from my perspective" or "Anybody who heard my story would believe me", but what a lot of people do not realize, especially when it involves their own issues, is there are at least two sides to every story. In court the difference is the judge sees it from the outside in, not the inside out.

I have come to realize that court does not meet the expectations of the people who appear there. Many people, especially in family law cases, want to be vindicated. They want the court to declare that they were right all along and their spouse was wrong. They want the judge to say that they are a better person and a better parent than their soon-to-be ex.

In the end, vindication is not my job. The court does not vindicate anyone. The judge is merely responsible for following the law, dividing the assets and debts of the marriage and making decisions about the best interest of the children. Nothing more, nothing less. Expecting anything more from the court is setting your expectations too high.

Summing Up

The family law court system in the United States is the best in the world. We have qualified, impartial judges making decisions about people's families. However, it has its flaws.

The system is designed to be adversarial. As an adversarial system it, by design, pits two sides against each other. When both parties cannot agree, they have to go to court and have a third-party decide their case. While the system is a fair one, the cost is rarely worth the benefit.

By reading this book you are on the right track. You know deep down that fighting is destructive for everyone. While emotions are running high, you know ultimately cooler heads will have to prevail. There is a place for an adversarial system of justice. Rarely is that place in the middle of families.

The following list summarizes the pros and cons of getting a divorce through a court trial. Later in the book, you'll see similar lists for each of the ADR methods we discuss. Use this information to compare your options and decide on the right course for you. Appendix B provides a side-by-side comparison between ADR and court trial. Appendix G provides greater information about Court Trial.

Court Trial (Litigated Divorce)

An adversarial system in which evidence is presented in court and a judge makes all decisions regarding the terms of the divorce.

(Continued)

Pluses

- Offers a last resort to have final decisions made and legally enforced if nothing else works.

- Courts can order and enforce protective orders in cases of domestic violence.

Minuses

- Courts are crowded, it could take several years to hear your case.

- Litigation is stressful, time consuming, and expensive.

- Some people try to use the courts to punish their spouse or as a public forum to complain about their spouse, wasting financial resources that would be better spent on the children's and spouses' future.

- You give up control over the outcome of your divorce to a complete stranger—a judge.

- Adversarial nature of the court system is likely to impair future relations with your spouse to resolve post-divorce disputes about children, alimony, etc.

- Discovery (gathering information for trial) is subject to strict rules and can be expensive, stressful, and time consuming.

4

The Costs of Divorce

The Pain of War cannot exceed the woe of the
aftermath.

Led Zeppelin

The cost of a divorce is substantial. And by cost, we don't just
mean the financial cost, which is significant, but also the emotional cost to you and your kids. In fact, these costs can even
span outside the immediate family to other family and friends.
If you have decided to divorce, we understand. You need to
keep the proper expectations and know that the overall cost of
divorce, especially a high conflict divorce, is sizable.

Financial Cost

Divorces cost a lot of money. From attorney's fees, other
professional fees, lost opportunity costs, increase in living
expenses, moving expenses, cost of dividing or selling property
and the loss of savings, divorce has a tangible negative impact
on a couple's finances.

In fact, divorce has been estimated to be between a $50-175 billion industry. By contrast, the wedding industry is estimated to generate $40-50 billion of business each year.

Attorney fees. The legal fees for a divorce can be staggering and is the most obvious expense. Attorney's fees alone in an uncontested, agreed divorce can range between a few thousand dollars to several thousands of dollars. In a contested, highly contentious divorce the total attorney's fees can be between $15,000 and several million dollars. Divorce lawyers charge between $200 and $1,000 or more per hour to represent clients. The more issues the attorney has to address, the more time it takes and the more you will be charged. You will be billed for every email, phone call, and face-to-face meeting, whether the contact is initiated by you or your spouse's attorney. Your lawyer will also charge you for drafting motions, correspondence, and any other time spent on your case. Even if some of the work is being done by paralegals or legal assistants, these professionals will set you back $75-250 an hour. You will also be billed for expenses such as filing fees, subpoena fees, copies, couriers, deposition fees, and much more.

Living expenses. But attorney's fees are not the only financial burden on a divorcing couple. Just think about it. You were struggling financially when you were together with one house payment, two car payments, one electric bill, one water bill, etc. When you separate or divorce you still have the same amount of money coming in the door, but now much more going out. Now you have two house/apartment payments, two electric bills, two phone bills, two water bills and, perhaps, child care—because you no longer cover the child care between yourselves—the list goes on and on. On top of the doubling of many bills, the amount spent on attorney's fees, child support, spousal support and other expenses related to divorce makes it very difficult to impossible to financially survive.

Costs of dividing property. Once you start dividing property the cost increases. For example, if you both need to sell your home in order to cash out the equity, you will pay real estate appraisal fees, realtor fees, costs to fix up the house for sale, taxes and other related expenses. The equity you thought you had in your house is diminished. Any equity realized from selling the house can quickly evaporate to pay for lease/mortgage deposits, utility deposits, new furniture (you only have half of the furniture you did have), dishes, TVs, pot pans, lawn mower, etc.

Retirement savings. The retirement account that you worked so hard for during the marriage is now subject to division. You can bet that the retirement account you will have left will be at least half the size it once was; the other half going to your spouse. If you have to cash the retirement out to help with these new expenses and obligations then you could suffer a tax consequence and a tax penalty.

As you can see, divorce is not cheap. It has serious financial impacts for all involved. In fact, the poverty rate for married couples is about 8% while the poverty rate for divorced couples is about 35%. Sixty percent of people under the poverty guidelines are divorced women and children. Divorce is the quickest way to poverty in the United States. We are not advocating for you to stay in a miserable marriage for financial reasons, but you need to fully understand the financial impact divorce will have for you and your family. The more effort you put in to a Divorce in Peace the more money you will retain for your future.

Emotional Costs for You

Divorce is a grieving process. There are a number of different theories on the number of stages of grief but fairly consistently they are: denial, anger, bargaining, depression and acceptance. The odd thing about divorce is that each of the people involved usually start the grieving process at different times, unlike grieving the death of a family member where everyone grieves at the same time. This, in turn, has the couple going through the grieving process in different stages, which can make the process more difficult and the ability to communicate even harder.

Women initiate divorce twice as much as men. This is usually a result of women being more in tune with marital problems. As these issues fester it can cause one of them to realize that the marriage is over while the other has no idea. The person who may have come to this realization earlier begins preparing for the separation and begins the grieving process. Privately, often with the other partner having no clue, the person starts the process of denial, anger, bargaining, and depression and has reached or will reach the level of acceptance. Once accepted the person announces to the oblivious partner that she wants a divorce, the other person is caught off guard and begins the grieving process. So while the first spouse has accepted the divorce the other starts the grieving process with denial, then anger (which makes matters worse), bargaining, depression, and sometime much later, acceptance. It's this overlapping process that creates so much conflict during a divorce.

What we hope is people realize this phenomenon and try to work through the emotions constructively before it gets out of hand.

Other emotional difficulties arise from losing family members and friends through the divorce. The parents of the divorcing couple take the side of their own son or daughter. The father-in-law who treats his son-in-law like his own withdraws from that friendship in solidarity with his daughter. The mother-in-law who you referred to as "Mom" backs away or, in the worst case scenario, assertively takes positions that are anti-you. The nieces and nephews withdraw from the in-law. Everyone begins the grieving process at different times causing a great deal of added stress.

Then there are your friends. Are they your friend or your spouse's friend? Why are they taking sides? The friends don't want to take sides or get involved at all and begin to withdraw. When you need your friends the most, many stay out of the way trying not to rock the boat. Often those friends start arguing within their own marriage as a result of them expressing their opinions about your divorce amongst themselves. You find yourself somewhat isolated from both family and friends. It's a vicious cycle.

Emotional Costs for Your Children

There is no doubt that divorce has a significant impact on children's present emotional health and can have an impact on a child's emotional development. Divorcing parents often minimize the potential impact of their divorce on their child by saying, "Kids are resilient. He is going to be fine." This is merely a justification of their current circumstance and is not reality.

While the kids have already been emotionally impacted by their parents' loveless marriage, the verbal fighting in the house and the obvious conflict between their parents, a divorce will be a huge change in the child's life at any age. Right from the start, one of his parents moves out of the family home and they are shuffled from one home to the other, only seeing one parent at a time.

While infants and toddlers will be affected by the divorce, the effects are less for them than for older children. Adolescents have an extremely difficult time coping with the divorce and their new life. They tend to withdraw from family and friends feeling caught in the middle by their parents and embarrassed in front of friends. This withdrawal tends to force the child to become prematurely independent. When children are interviewed by a judge in the middle of a divorce, it is strikingly obvious that these children mature at an earlier age. This is a product of the required early independence a child obtains in an attempt to try to stay neutral in the divorce and keeping their own emotions and problems to themselves. They try desperately not to burden their parents who are going through a divorce.

Divorce changes everything a child knows about marriage, relationships and family. Many times a parent tries to comfort the child, so they think, by explaining the divorce and why it happens. They tell their side of the story, which is just that—their side of the story.

Kids often report how it hurts them when one parent talks badly about the other parent. They know that they are a product of half their mom and half their dad. If one parent thinks that bad about the other parent, how must that parent think of them? It is very confusing, upsetting and painful for the child to hear bad things about one parent from the other. The child loves them both no matter what is going on. This emotional toll can have both short- and long-term effects.

In the most extreme circumstances, a parent purposefully

tries to alienate the child from the other parent. One 10 year old boy was asked why he didn't like his dad. He said it was because his father had been kicked out of the Army and was fired from his last job. The boy also explained that he called his father by his first name because he had not earned the title of "Dad." These aren't reasons a 10 year old would give. The mother had obviously told the boy these things in an attempt to distance him from his father. This is an awful tactic, but is used much more than you would hope by both mothers and fathers.

The Cost of Fighting

Divorce has financial and emotional costs, and if the process is turned into a war, the costs escalate. The more you argue and battle over the issues, the more time the attorneys will have to spend on your case and the more fees you'll have to pay them. The greater the fight, the greater the cost.

Let's assume you and your spouse's net worth is $200,000. The equitable division of the money would give each spouse $100,000. However, if you can convince a judge that your spouse is at fault for the breakup of the marriage—it is very difficult, if not impossible, to determine who exactly is at fault—you might get a disproportionate or larger share. Can you, despite knowing what judges see every day, convince this judge you deserve 60% of the $200,000—$120,000? If so, you could have a net benefit of $20,000.

How much are you willing to pay in legal fees to find out if your prediction is right or wrong? Remember, attorney's fees usually come out of the gross marital assets. It will take money to fight about it. At the end of the day, you can still lose—meaning you spend more than was originally necessary to fight over the possibility of getting more. If you don't convince the judge to see it your way, and you and your spouse spent $20,000 on attorney's fees fighting about it, your individual take is now $90,000. For what?

The most incredible thing about this situation is it's so common. It's not unusual for people to spend more money than they could ever get in court. In fact, many people have a negative net worth, meaning they owe more than the value of their assets. They are fighting over a disproportionate share—a lesser share—of the debts. All the while, the couple is getting further in debt because of the legal fees. Not smart, but not unusual.

Clients oftentimes cash in their retirement accounts, college funds, and other assets to help fund their fight for a greater piece of the pie. Ultimately, these financial sacrifices and efforts result in them receiving much less than when they originally started because now there is nothing left.

Of course, fighting over the divorce also increases the emotional cost to you and your children. You are already coping with sorrow and stress. Anger and conflict make the situation worse.

Fighting for Your Children

In our experience, the biggest and most expensive divorce cases are those involving children. The woman with whom the man made a conscious decision to have a baby with is now Mommy Dearest. The father who was so involved, who took care of the kids when Mom went on work trips, now is so incompetent that the visits with the children should be supervised. Once the judge sees Dad's incompetence, surely the judge will order restrictions on his visitation.

Judges spend their days listening to these types of allegations. In many states and counties, judges who hear divorce cases also hear cases involving Child Protective Services where the allegations against the parents are so severe that the government asks the court to remove those children from both of their parents and put them in foster care. Now, the judge calls your case and has a hearing on the allegations in your case—mom's against dad and dad's against mom. And you believe you can convince the judge your spouse is so bad that their visitation with their kids should be restricted? Often times this can even backfire on the initiating parent.

Certainly there are cases where the court will limit the other parent's visitation with the kids. The most common cases we see are when one of the parents is addicted to drugs or alcohol. Restrictive orders are put in place to protect the child, but usually these orders are temporary. In these types of cases, the court will impose restrictions on the offending parent such as drug testing, psychological evaluations, etc., and then revisit the issue. Even if the parent has tested positive for drugs and the court orders supervised visitation, the court's ultimate goal is for the parent to get their act together so visitation restrictions can be lifted. While it's not the result you might want, having a healthy, involved parent is good for the kids.

Frankly, in the court system we often tell parents the Court doesn't care what looks good for the parents among their friends or what might be best for them. Rather, the Court cares what's best for the children. What is best for their children is having a healthy, productive, caring relationship with both parents.

Judge's Perspective
Is It Worth the Cost?

I had one case in my court that was very contentious. The couple had been fighting for years and spent thousands of dollars already. In fact, it had been going on for so long that my dad was a judge over the case at some point, and my dad has been retired for over 15 years. Imagine that: Kids caught in the crossfire for so long it lasted through two generations of the judge's family.

They appeared before me wanting the court to modify the existing orders concerning the children. At this point, we had already had several hearings on discovery issues. The parents painstakingly went through the past, used the opportunity to bash the other parent, and paid their lawyers to try to convince me the other parent was bad.

At the conclusion of the hearing, I asked both parties how much each of them had paid in legal fees over the last 15 years. Dad answered he had spent $120,000. Mom responded she had spent about $95,000. These folks did not have that type of money lying around.

I asked them whether the perpetual litigation and gorging of money for the child's entire life had made an overall improvement in their child's life. They said, embarrassed, "No". I further expounded on the point by asking them, "If you had put all this money away and allowed the money grow for the child's education, would that have been more of a benefit?" As expected, they responded, "Yes." They finally agreed on something!

(continued)

I withheld my decision on the case, and I advised them I wanted them to finally grow up and work together to get these issues resolved by the people who are in the best position to make these decisions for the child—them. I ordered them to sit down in a restaurant together, discuss the matter, and get it resolved. I was happy to learn several days later they had reached an agreement. It's my hope I never see these people again.

Summing Up

We hope you realize the extreme cost of war. The more you fight, the more devastating war actually is. For the sake of yourself, your children, and your finances, please understand the full cost of divorce, both financially and emotionally. Recognize that the effects of divorce extend beyond your immediate family, to your extended family and your friends.

If divorce is still the option you choose, do not make it more devastating than it has to be. Critically analyze whether your expectations of fighting it out in court are realistic—whether the potential benefit is worth the financial and emotional cost. Our prediction is that in most circumstances, the answer is *no*.

Instead of going to war with your spouse, choose peace. Try the ADR methods described in this book. Be a responsible adult and make business decisions about your finances. Your financial future depends on it. Be a responsible parent and work hard to understand the impact the divorce is having on your children. Do everything you can to insulate your children from the divorce and keep conflict to a minimum. Your children deserve it. You deserve to Divorce in Peace.

5

Alternative Dispute Resolution: An Overview

Sometimes, God doesn't send you into a battle
to win it; he sends you to end it.

Shannon L. Adler

If you have tried all you can to save your marriage, and you still think that divorce is your best option, you are faced with another important choice. Will you take the traditional, adversarial approach to divorce, or will you find a more productive way to end your marriage? Alternative Dispute Resolution gives you a path to a peaceful divorce.

The Purpose of ADR

Every divorce brings a host of issues that need to be dealt with: division of property, spousal and child support, child custody, and more. Alternative Dispute Resolution (ADR) allows you and your spouse to resolve these issues without going through an adversarial court trial.

Even if you decide to use ADR, you can't avoid court altogether. You (or your attorney) will still have to file certain paperwork and make a brief court appearance. The key is that with ADR, you can reach an agreement by negotiating with one another, rather than letting the court decide the destiny of your money and your children.

ADR Methods

ADR offers a choice of several methods. They range from simple and informal options to more structured, formal processes.

The IHOP method. The least formal approach is to simply discuss the issues with your spouse and reach an agreement that satisfies you both. We call this method "Informal, Healthy Opportunity for Peace," or IHOP. The acronym is appropriate, because you can begin this process by sitting down together at an IHOP restaurant, for example, and talk things over.

Mediation. This option adds a neutral third party—a qualified family law mediator—to help you resolve your issues. You and your spouse, your lawyers (if you wish), and the mediator will meet in one or more sessions to discuss the issues, brainstorm about solutions, and reach an agreement.

Collaborative Law. In this method, each spouse is represented by an attorney who is trained and experienced in Collaborative Law. Rather than battle each other, both spouses and both attorneys work together to resolve the issues surrounding the divorce in a team approach.

Arbitration. Instead of using the public court system, couples can hire a private judge to serve as an arbitrator. Each spouse is represented by an attorney and presents evidence. The arbitrator makes the final decision. This option is less cooperative than the other ADR methods, but it is quicker, often less expensive, and more private than using the public court system.

The chapters in Part Two go into more detail about each of these ADR options.

Advantages of ADR

ADR is appealing for many reasons, and offers many advantages over a court trial.

Less emotional cost. Court is an adversarial process, with winners and losers. By nature, ADR is cooperative rather than combative. By agreeing to work together, you and your spouse can lessen the emotional damage to yourselves and your children.

Less financial cost. If you've read Chapter 4, you already know how expensive a court trial can be. ADR allows you to save money by reducing attorney fees and avoiding the delays and repeated hearings of a litigated divorce.

More creativity. In a court trial, judges have very specific rules they must follow. These rules, as well as time constraints caused by an overcrowded court system, can limit the judge's ability to provide creative solutions tailored to meet a couple's specific needs. In an ADR setting, there are fewer rules restricting the creativity of the solutions. There is more time to fully analyze specific issues and come up with free-flowing, creative solutions.

More control. Going to court is risky. The results are unpredictable. ADR gives you more control over the ultimate outcome. Instead of letting a judge make all the decisions that determine your future, you and your spouse negotiate and reach a mutual decision.

More privacy. If you get your divorce through a public

court trial, anyone can come to the courtroom and watch. Furthermore, all the documents you present as evidence and all the transcripts of what you say in court are public records that anyone can see. With ADR, you conduct your negotiations in a private setting. The only public document is the Final Decree/Order.

Greater satisfaction. Finally, studies indicate that couples who successfully resolve their issues through an ADR process are more likely to be satisfied with the results than those who participate in full litigation. Also, compared to orders made by a judge, agreements made in ADR are less likely to be brought back to court for future disputes.

Does ADR Work?

You may be thinking that there is no way you can sit down with your spouse and have a constructive conversation to resolve your issues. You fight too much or are so angry at each other that you couldn't possibly resolve your divorce issues without going to court.

Most of the time, this isn't true. Over 90% of divorce cases filed with a court are settled outside of court, either by the couples on their own or through the use of an ADR method.

ADR doesn't leave you high and dry to do it on your own. You can decide whether and when to get help from professionals. Family Law mediators and Collaborative Law attorneys are trained and experienced in discussing these issues in a productive manner. They choose appropriate mediation techniques based on your present ability to communicate. They are well equipped to handle your conflicts. Keep in mind that Family Law often involves high conflict, so your situation is not unique. With very few exceptions, you cannot come up with a situation that an experienced Family Law mediator or attorney hasn't seen.

Also, remember that ADR methods can be helpful even if they don't lead to a complete settlement. For example, you and your spouse might use the IHOP method to resolve issues surrounding your finances, but use another method to reach an agreement on child custody and visitation. Or you might reach an agreement on most of the issues using ADR and submit the remaining issues for the court to decide. With that said, the goal should be a full and final agreement.

Judge's Perspective
The Differences Are Obvious

One of the wonders in life is that you never know what might have been. When you make a decision you never know what would have happened if you would have made the alternate decision. For example, if you litigated your divorce in court and had the court make all the decisions, you would never know the benefits of an ADR process. Likewise, if you settled your case using an ADR process, you would never know how much of a benefit that process was to your emotional or financial health. From my perspective, I see the difference every day.

Whether a couple resolves their divorce with an agreement or litigates their case in court, they have to see the judge to make the divorce official. As a result, I have seen thousands and thousands of couples who have come to court to have their divorce declared official.

(continued)

I see couples who have settled their cases between themselves, in Mediation, Collaborative Law or in Arbitration. For those who have not settled their case, I am the judge making the decision about their divorce. The comparison of the parties' reaction to the finalization of their divorce is starkly different.

For those who have a contested divorce trial in my court, I might have heard hours of evidence about their various disputes. I have heard all about their property and how they want it divided. I have heard hours about their children, their parenting styles, the good and bad about each parent and, sometimes, I have actually interviewed the child in my office without parents or attorneys. Both parties feel they have provided evidence to support their side. Their positions are righteous. They have invested a considerable amount of time, money and emotions for this moment in time.

As they await my decision the look of distress is obvious. My decision is important to them and I know my decision will make a significant impact on their lives, the lives of their friends and families, their finances and their children. I do not relish this part of the job. As I begin to pronounce my verdict the hammer drops quickly. I see the disappointment on their faces. The final realization of how their lives have changed forever. One decision after another takes its toll on both of them. No one leaves the courtroom happy. Divorce is not a happy occasion. Court is not a happy place. Losing control over the outcome of our own lives leaves one empty, disappointed and helpless.

I'm not saying people who decide to settle their divorces

(continued)

outside of court are happy. That is not the case. But they do come to court to finalize their cases with what appears to be more optimism about their futures. Couples who come to court together sometimes cry. Others are very business-like. They are not happy to be divorced, they may not even be happy with the deal they made with each other. They seem to be more satisfied than anything else. I suppose they are satisfied that this phase of their life is over and they maintained control of how it ended.

It is always my hope for all the couples who appear before me that they move on with a happy and healthy life and that their kids will, too. However, I see those who litigated their cases in my court more often coming back to court with more issues than those who settled their cases out of court, spending more money and wasting more time. Settle your case outside of court. You will be glad you did.

Use ADR Sooner Rather Than Later

It's important to understand that even if you go through the court system, you will likely be required to use an ADR process, like Mediation, before taking up the court's time in trial. Courts routinely make this requirement to help ease their ever growing dockets, and it has proven to work very well.

In many cases, however, Mediation and other useful ADR processes are not employed until just before trial. If you wait until the week before trial to participate in court-ordered mediation as a last-minute effort to settle, you're likely to miss out on many of ADR's benefits. By then the damage to your relationship with your soon-to-be ex-spouse has been done; your children will have been through the turmoil of litigation; the lawyers will have all been paid, and that money is gone. Using one or more of the ADR options early in the divorce process, can help to resolve your issues sooner rather than later.

Knowing this, why not try ADR? The worst that could happen is that you fail to resolve the issues and go about your divorce through the courts. The best that could happen is that you settle your case with less conflict and without spending great sums of money.

How to Get Started

Before using ADR to settle your agreements, you and your spouse must first agree to use ADR. Perhaps you are already at that point and are reading this book together. On the other hand, you may be reading this book while your spouse is arming for war. Or you may not even have told your spouse you want a divorce.

When the topic of divorce first comes up, emotions run high. Conversations often break down quickly, with one or both spouses invoking phrases like, "You will hear from my lawyer," "I will take every penny you have," or "I will make sure you will never see your kids again." After a cool-down period, perhaps you can convince your spouse to approach the situation a little differently. Maybe you can provide a copy of this book. You might also send your spouse a link to our webpage at www.divorceinpeace.com, which explains the Divorce in Peace concept. No matter how you decide to broach the subject, try not to slip into the roles of warriors.

Once you have agreed to use ADR, this book can guide

your way. As you read the chapters in Part Two, examine each of the various ADR methods and consider their pros and cons. Together with your spouse, determine which method to use based on your expectations, goals, and preferences. If you're not sure, you can try the least intrusive method, IHOP, first. If that doesn't work, move on to the next method until you find one you are comfortable with, that is better suited for the two of you.

Summing Up

Statistics show divorces that are settled between the parties rather than decided by the court have less of a chance of coming back to court. In other words, cases decided by a judge are more likely to return to court when future disputes arise. This is a result of the parties never having learned how to communicate about their issues. They didn't communicate well during the marriage, the communication got worse during the divorce and certainly it has not and will not get better without the help of professionals.

On the other hand those who have had to learn to communicate, can make adjustments in their positions and expectations, work hard on finding common ground and, ultimately, have at least the foundation on how to communicate about issues regarding their family.

You won't know how ADR processes will benefit your current situation until you try. In the end, you may or may not be happy about getting divorced, but you will at least have had the opportunity to maintain control of your divorce issues and preserve your financial security as best you can.

Part Two

Understanding ADR Methods

6

The IHOP Method

Don't dwell on what went wrong. Instead, focus on what to do next. Spend your energies on moving forward toward finding the answer.

Denis Waitley

You've probably heard of IHOP, especially if you're a fan of pancakes and maple syrup. In this chapter, however, IHOP has a different meaning. It's an acronym for Informal, Healthy Opportunity for Peace. We believe this ADR method can be the most fruitful way to end up with a peaceful divorce.

Start with Coffee

Here's how the IHOP method works. When you and your spouse decide to divorce, we recommend that both of you go to IHOP—and this time we mean the restaurant, or some other public place. Have a cup of coffee, breakfast, lunch, or dinner and begin to discuss the issues that now confront the two of you.

Why meet in a restaurant? There is really no good place to discuss a divorce, but in a public place, the conversation is more likely to stay civil and calm. It's also important to be away from the kids while you talk.

You won't resolve all of the issues in one conversation, of course. Over time, as you continue to meet with one another, you will discuss each issue in turn. If all goes well, you will eventually reach a mutually satisfactory agreement.

Some of you may think this is absolutely impossible. After all, if you and your spouse could communicate easily and civilly, this divorce wouldn't be happening. With the proper ground rules in place and with an agenda in mind, the IHOP method can be an effective way of settling disputes. Besides, if you don't learn to communicate with each other about these important issues now, you will have to communicate through your lawyers. The former approach will be much more productive and less expensive. The latter will not only be expensive, but will likely put the relationship in an unsalvageable position.

You may be thinking there is absolutely nothing to salvage, and from a relationship perspective, you're probably right. But if you're not careful, you're likely to waste away any financial security the two of you have created during your marriage. You're also likely to negatively, and perhaps permanently, impact your kids' childhood and perhaps their adult lives. So in approaching your divorce, realize that you need to confront the task with level heads. Yes, that's easier said than done, but in the long run it's easier to take this approach rather than the combative one.

The Initial Meeting

If you decide to try the IHOP method, you may wonder where to begin. As explained in Chapter 2, certain preliminary steps need to be taken in any divorce. These are appropriate topics for your initial meeting.

First, you could discuss who will file for divorce and when. After filing, the other spouse will sign a Waiver of Service. Chapter 2 describes how to complete these steps.

This may be a good time to begin talking about your family finances. Do both of you have a clear sense of your financial picture? What information should be gathered and shared, such as a listing of accounts and balances? Should you make each other copies of financial documents or digital files? What questions do each of you have for the other?

You might also discuss the temporary agreements that you'll follow until the divorce is finalized. These are the equivalent of the temporary orders that would be issued by a judge if the divorce went to court. You'll need to decide who will live where while the divorce is in process, and who will pay which bills. If you have children, you'll need to reach temporary agreement on where the kids will live, how often they will visit the other parent, whether child support payments should start now, and if so the amount. If you can't reach a consensus in your first meeting, at least identify these issues and plan to address them at another time.

Your initial meeting will give you a better idea of how well you communicate with each other. You will also begin to realize which decisions will be easier to agree on and which may be more difficult. You can use these insights to plan your future meetings.

What Are the Issues?

During the divorce process, you and your spouse will need to address many issues. The list below will provide a general idea of what you'll need to agree on. A more detailed checklist can be found in Appendix I.

Real property. If you and your spouse own a home, you are faced with many questions. Will it be sold, or will one of you keep it? How much is it worth, and how will that value be divided between you? What about the mortgage, taxes, repairs, refinancing, and other issues? Any other real property you own, such as rental units or land, will also require discussion and agreement.

Personal property. Possessions such as vehicles, furniture, collectibles, and equipment will need to be divided between you or sold.

Financial assets. Bank accounts, retirement accounts, pension plans, life insurance, stocks, and other investments will also need to be allocated between you.

Debts. You'll need to decide who will be responsible for credit card debt, personal loans, auto loans, and other joint debts.

Income tax. Issues here may include refunds, taxes owed, and filing status.

Spousal support. In many cases, a divorced spouse who earns less or has been a stay-at-home parent receives support payments from the other spouse. If this fits your situation, you'll need to agree on the monthly amount and how long payments will continue.

Child support and expenses. With few exceptions, both parents are responsible for providing for their children's financial needs. Therefore, if you have kids, you'll need to decide which parent will make child support payments to the other, in what amount, and when and how they will be paid. Aside from support payments, you may need to plan for college savings, medical coverage, and other expenses.

Child custody. This issue includes not only where your children will primarily live, but who has the legal right to make certain decisions about their welfare.

Visitation schedules. You'll need to plan how much time children will spend with each parent and when, including weekdays, weekends, holidays, and summer.

Other parenting issues. You may want to discuss restrictions that will apply when a parent is in possession of the children, such as not using alcohol around the kids or not spending the night with a romantic partner.

The list of issues seems daunting, to say the least. So each time you meet, choose one or two specific topics. Do not try to tackle all of them at once. During your first few meetings, you may want to start with whatever topics seem easier for you and your spouse to talk about. As you become more practiced at communicating and reaching agreement, you can move on to more contentious and emotional issues. In Part Three of this book, you can read about common approaches to resolving the issues involved in a divorce.

Five Ground Rules

When using the IHOP process—or any of the other ADR methods—your chances of success will be greater if you follow these ground rules:

Rule 1: Stay focused on the goal for the day. Each time you and your spouse meet, set a mutual goal to accomplish. Even so, the natural inclination will be to bring up other topics, past history, or other people's situations. When this happens, call a time out and get back to the issue you agreed to focus on.

Rule 2: Clarify before you crucify. We all tend to make assumptions about what another person is saying. In fact, we often fail to actually listen completely. We get hung up on something too early in the conversation and let our minds fill in the rest. This is not helpful for effective communication. If you think your spouse just slammed you, your family, and everything else you believe in, ask your spouse to restate what was said. You may have heard it right, but chances are, you may have heard something that your spouse did not actually say or mean.

Rule 3: Be respectful. You are both grown up enough to address these issues as adults. Do not let the conversation go down the tubes in an atmosphere of disrespect. Your futures are too important. Your children's futures are too important.

Rule 4: Agree to disagree. You won't get very far in your discussions if you keep insisting, "I'm right and you're wrong!" This is not the time to point out the error of your spouse's ways. Simply accept the fact that you and your spouse have different ideas, and move on to finding something you *can* agree on.

Rule 5: Reach enthusiastic agreement on the issue. As discussed in Rule 4, it will be almost impossible to convince your spouse to see it your way. But there is more than one way to solve a problem. It does not have to be "my way" or "your way." Make it "our way." Keep thinking outside of the box until you reach a resolution that you are both enthusiastic about.

All of these ground rules are important. The most crucial, however, is Rule 5. We learned the concept of "mutually enthusiastic agreement" from Willard F. Harley's book *His Needs, Her Needs.* This rule is the essence of agreement. Learn to use it the best you can.

Mediator's Perspective
Both of You Can Win

Rule 5 tells you to reach an agreement that both you and your spouse are enthusiastic about. Here's an example of how a couple could successfully follow this rule. The example is not about divorce, but the rule works in any situation.

Michelle wanted her family—her husband David and their three kids, all under the age of five—to take her parents on a family vacation. Sounds good in theory, but there were a few complications. Michelle's dad was 70 years old and had recently been diagnosed with a blood disorder. As if that wasn't enough, he had recently fallen off a roof and broken his back. Michelle's idea was the family should all go to Disney World for the vacation of a lifetime.

Michelle's husband, David, didn't think this was such a great idea. He knew that Michelle's dad would struggle through the theme park in the heat. Under the circumstances, David thought going on a family vacation was out of the question. His first impulse was to tell Michelle, "No way!"

Here's where Rule 5 comes into play. Instead of jumping into the ring for a boxing match between "Disney World" and "no vacation," David realized that he and Michelle needed to come up with a plan they both felt enthusiastic about. David thought about what Michelle was actually trying to accomplish. He could see she wanted her parents, who live out of state, to have quality time with their kids. How could he help make this happen?

(Continued)

David did some research to find other vacation options that might work out better for their kids and her parents. The one that appealed to David most was a cruise. The ship would have things for him and Michelle to do, things for the kids to do, things for her parents to do, and things they could all do together. David pictured the four adults relaxing on lounge chairs by the pool, watching the kids swim. This kind of vacation seemed much more doable.

The couple sat down together to talk things over. David started by saying that he completely understood and agreed with Michelle's desire for her parents to spend more time with their kids. He also explained why he thought Disney World was not a good choice. Michelle listened carefully and agreed that a theme park might be too challenging for her dad. David then asked, "What would you think about taking a cruise instead?" Michelle studied the information David had gathered about accommodations, activities, and price. She saw the possibilities and pointed out a few drawbacks. Together they discussed the pros and cons. With respectful consideration of each other's viewpoints, they eventually came to an enthusiastic agreement: they would go on the cruise.

Case Study: Visitation Schedule

Now let's look at an example of how these ground rules apply in the IHOP method. In keeping with Rule 1, the spouses begin the session by restating their previously agreed goal: to figure out an appropriate visitation schedule.

Dad begins the discussion. He proposes a schedule in which he will have the kids one week and Mom will have them the next week. They will exchange the kids at 6 p.m. on Sunday. "That makes everything perfectly equal," he says.

Mom shakes her head. "That won't work. I have something else in mind." She outlines a visitation schedule: Dad gets the kids every other weekend, from 6 p.m. Friday to 6 p.m. Sunday, and four weeks during the summer.

Dad listens, but starts to get a little angry. He has always been a very involved parent. He should have equal time with the kids, and what his spouse proposed isn't even close! *She's trying to keep the kids away from me*, a voice inside him whispers. *She thinks I'm a bad parent.*

Instead of lashing back at her, Dad remembers Rule 2: Clarify before you crucify. He takes a deep, calming breath, "Can you tell me why you think the schedule I asked for won't work?"

Mom is tempted to give a sarcastic reply, "Are you out of your mind?" But she follows Rule 3 by staying respectful. She explains that she doesn't want to go seven days without seeing her kids. Also, Dad tends to travel a lot with work and is gone one or two nights a week. This could significantly interfere with the kids' routines and school activities.

Dad admits that Mom is right about his work travel, and like Mom, he doesn't want to be away from his kids seven days in a row. But he explains he still thinks Mom's proposed schedule won't let him spend enough time with his kids.

Mom understands, but doesn't know what else to suggest. The conversation seems stuck. Finally Mom comments, "It seems like we have very different ideas about what schedule would work best." Rule 4: Agree to disagree.

As they talk further, they come to realize their goals are

exactly the same. They both want to spend as much time with the kids as possible. They also agree kids tend to thrive on a regular schedule and their schooling is important.

Having found common ground, the parents evaluate more options. They consider a 50-50 schedule in which Dad would have the kids every Monday and Tuesday, Mom would have them every Wednesday and Thursday, and they would alternate weekends. But after talking it over, they agree this back-and-forth schedule would be too rough on the kids' daily routines, schoolwork, and emotional stability.

They come up with a schedule they can both agree on, after much dialogue, patience, and listening. Dad will have the kids every other weekend. But instead of starting on Friday, the weekend will begin on Thursday after school. And instead of returning the kids to Mom on Sunday evening, Dad will take them to school on Monday morning. In addition, Dad will have the kids for five weeks in the summer. Mom and Dad will alternate holidays, except that Mom will always get the kids on Mother's Day weekend and Dad will have them on Father's Day weekend.

The parents realize their goals have been met. They enthusiastically agree this schedule is the best option for the kids and for themselves.

It won't always work out this well, but give it a try. The worst you could do is agree to disagree and move forward with one of the other dispute resolution processes. The best case is that you and your spouse reach full agreement using IHOP. By doing so, you avoid war and leave your livelihood and children in the hands of people you trust—yourselves.

Write an Agreement

If all goes well, during each IHOP session you and your spouse will reach enthusiastic agreement on a specific issue. At the end of the session, write down what you have decided that day. Once you have discussed and resolved all the issues, you will compile your decisions into a final written agreement.

Be as detailed as possible. For example, in addition to specifying which spouse will be responsible for credit card debt, write down "credit card debt from Bank of America" and include the last four digits of the account number. The more specific the agreement is, the better you will both understand your expectations of each other, and the better you will be able to communicate in the future.

See an Attorney

You have done your best to get this divorce done. You think your written agreement covers everything and you are protected. However, a little voice in your head makes you hesitant to sign any agreement with your spouse. That is perfectly understandable and very smart of you. At this point, it is advisable for you, and your spouse, to see an attorney.

You may be thinking, "What? I bought this book and chose the IHOP method to resolve my divorce issues because I did not want lawyers involved!" Let us explain.

You can hire a lawyer for the limited purpose of advising you on specific issues; terms that describe this situation include "consulting attorney," "limited purpose," and "limited-scope representation." This is not the same as hiring an attorney to take your divorce to court.

In the case of your IHOP agreement, the consulting attorney will simply review the agreement and advise you of your options. You want the attorney to explain what you are giving up and what you are getting, as well as make sure that you and your spouse have covered all the bases. Your spouse may also want to hire a consulting attorney to do the same thing. If your spouse does want to consult an attorney as well, the attorney will need to be a completely different attorney than the one you hired. The attorneys should charge for only a couple of hours of their time.

Where can you find such an attorney? On our website, www.divorceinpeace.com, look for the Divorce in Peace Attorney Network. This section lists attorneys who have pledged to follow the concepts and ideas of a peaceful divorce. They have each received this book and are committed to helping you achieve your goals. Chapter 15 explains more about how to hire a lawyer.

Any attorney you hire to review your agreement has a legal obligation to inform you that you could go to court instead. However, be wary if the attorney says you are getting screwed and could do so much better in court. If this happens, ask how much the attorney would charge to take your divorce to trial. The amount will be in the thousands. Go find another lawyer for a second opinion, then make up your own mind about whether you are satisfied with the outcome of your agreement.

Once the attorneys have reviewed your agreement and you are satisfied with the terms, you and your spouse can sign it. We recommend that you print and sign two copies, one for you and one for your spouse.

Finalize the Divorce

After you have signed the agreement, you may think that everything is done—case over. Not so fast. You are not officially divorced yet. For example, you can't just send your agreement to your bank to have your spouse's name removed from the bank account, and you can't send your agreement to the school to let them know which parent can pick up the kids on what days. The bank, school, employers, and governmental departments and agencies will need a copy of a Final Decree/Order that has been signed by a judge. You or an attorney will need to draft the Final Decree/Order, which should include all the agreements that you reached. Chapter 16 explains how to finalize your divorce.

Summing Up

We truly believe IHOP is one of the best methods that a couple could possibly use to get a peaceful divorce. Still, it will not be easy. Don't give up too soon. Remember that at one time, you got along well enough to get married. Even though your marriage did not work out, you *can* get along well enough to Divorce in Peace. Press forward.

However, it's possible that in the end, you and your spouse won't be able to resolve all of your issues using IHOP. What then? Please don't get angry, lawyer up, and fight it out in court. Simply try another ADR process, such as Mediation or Collaborative Law, and see what you can accomplish with help from legal professionals.

IHOP
(Informal, Healthy Opportunity for Peace)

Voluntary negotiation between spouses without the use of lawyers or mediators; based on ground rules and an agenda to resolve issues.

Pluses

- Private process; no court transcripts.

- Gives you and your spouse total control.

- Least expensive way to avoid a divorce war; preserves assets for you, your spouse, and your children's future.

- Improves chances that you and your spouse will remain on speaking terms after the divorce.

- Promotes communication techniques that can help you resolve any post-divorce disputes.

- Costs nothing to try; other ADR options are still open if you can't agree.

Minuses

- No mediators or lawyers to guide your discussions or help you resolve issues.

- Requires discipline and rigid adherence to ground rules.

(Continued)

· Doesn't work if spouses are unable to leave their rants at home and focus on the issues.

· Not recommended if one or both spouses are engaging in family violence or other illegal conduct.

7

Mediation

Believe it is possible to solve your problem. Tremendous things happen to the believer. So believe the answer will come. It will.

Norman Vincent Peale

Perhaps you and your spouse have tried the IHOP method but were unable to settle all of your differences. Or perhaps you know your situation well enough to see that IHOP will not work for you. But you don't want a bitter, contentious divorce, nor do you want to spend a significant amount of money on legal fees. Mediation might be the best option for you.

What Is Mediation?

Mediation is a process in which a neutral third party—a mediator—helps people settle their disputes. It is the most commonly used form of ADR, not just in divorces but in all types of cases and controversies. It is widely accepted by family law courts all over the country as an effective process that is solution-based, not adversarial.

Mediation is usually a voluntary process, but because of its proven success, many courts require Mediation before a divorce case goes to trial. In other words, if you and your spouse go through the lengthy court process to get a divorce, you will eventually end up in Mediation. Our feeling is that if you're going to use Mediation at some point, why not try it sooner rather than later? If you don't settle the first time, you can always go back and try it again, or move on to another ADR method.

The Mediator's Role

The key to Mediation is the mediator. The role of the mediator is not to make the decisions about your divorce or to tell you what decisions to make. Rather, the mediator is a trained facilitator who can help you and your spouse come to an agreement. The mediator may suggest options for you to consider, but you and your spouse maintain control of the ultimate outcome.

A mediator has the skills and training to:

- Listen to each spouse's viewpoints and concerns.
- Identify the issues.
- Frame the issues so everyone can understand them.
- Clarify each spouse's goals.
- Help spouses find common ground.
- Suggest possible options for resolving the issues.
- Assist in negotiations.

In short, mediators are very effective at helping you and your spouse reach a mutually satisfying agreement. That's true even if you come to the table with major disputes about significant issues. By the nature of their business, family law mediators are quite accustomed to conflict. They have specialized knowledge in communication skills and in dealing with the emotions of divorce.

Choosing a Mediator

You and your spouse will want to choose a qualified, experienced family law mediator. Do your research to find good candidates. Ask knowledgeable people, such as family law attorneys and marriage counselors, for recommendations. You can also look for mediators in your area at www.divorceinpeace.com.

When you have identified a potential mediator, make an appointment for an initial consultation. Both you and your spouse should attend. Some questions you may want to ask are:

What is your training and experience? Mediators are not licensed by the state or any other governmental body, but some have received certification through training courses or professional associations. Ask about the number of cases the mediator has handled and the overall success rate. Make sure you choose a mediator with experience in cases that involve the same types of issues you are facing.

How do you conduct your mediations? As you will learn later in the chapter, mediators can take different approaches. Ask about the number and length of sessions and whether you and your spouse will be in the same room or different rooms. If you feel more comfortable with one mediation style over another, let the mediator know. At the same time, remember to trust the mediator's professional judgment.

How much do you charge? The mediator may charge by the hour, half day, or full day. Ask if there are additional costs, such as an extra charge for drafting the final agreement. Find out whether you need to pay in advance. Some mediators ask for a retainer fee as a deposit, while others require all fees up front.

While these are the "must ask" questions, another important factor is what you and your spouse think of the prospective mediator. Are you both comfortable with the mediator's style and personality? Do you trust this person to guide you through the process? If you answer "yes" and are satisfied with what the mediator has told you, then you can feel confident in choosing this person.

Agreement to Mediate

When you and your spouse are ready to proceed, you will be asked to sign an Agreement to Mediate. This agreement will:

- Outline the process for mediation.
- Explain the confidentiality of the process.
- Confirm your understanding that the mediator, if an attorney, is not representing either spouse and will not give you legal advice.
- Advise you of your right to consult with outside legal counsel during or at the end of the process.
- Disclose the fees associated with the mediation.

Should You BYOA (Bring Your Own Attorney)?

If you wish, you and your spouse may each hire your own attorney to attend Mediation with you. The attorney will advise you about your options and ensure that your legal rights are upheld. This provides more protection than simply having an attorney review the final agreement after Mediation is completed.

If your situation is complicated, you may want an attorney to represent you through the entire divorce process, from the time the divorce is filed until it is finally granted by the court. While this is not necessary, you should do so if you feel the issues are too difficult for you to handle on your own.

Another option is to hire an attorney on a Limited-Scope Representation basis, meaning the attorney will do only the tasks that you request. If you go this route, you can hire the attorney to represent you in the mediation process itself or simply to review the proposed final agreement after it is hammered out. Limited-Scope Representation costs less than full representation. You will have to balance that advantage against the drawback of having to go through some of the divorce process alone. Also remember you can initially hire an attorney on a limited basis and see how it works out. If you feel you need more legal help, you can hire the attorney to represent you through the remainder of the process.

Whatever option you choose, be sure you find an attorney who has experience with Mediation and understands the process. The worst thing you could do is hire a lawyer who escalates the situation to the point where war begins. You can find attorneys who adhere to the Divorce in Peace principles at www.divorceinpeace.com. Chapter 15 provides more information about hiring an attorney.

Additional Experts

During your initial consultation, or later in the process, the mediator may discuss the possibility of including additional experts in some of the mediation sessions. For example, suppose one of your children has been diagnosed with ADHD, and you and your spouse disagree about the best plan for treatment. A medical doctor could educate both of you, as well as the mediator, on the different options that are available. Similarly, a realtor or real estate appraiser could help determine the value of your home and how fast it might sell. A CPA could explain the tax implications of cashing in a 401k or stocks.

At this point you might be saying, "Bringing in experts sounds expensive." It's true that it will increase the cost of Mediation, but doing so can help you, your spouse, and the mediator resolve the issues more quickly. Besides, if you went to court instead of using Mediation, both you and your spouse would need to hire your own experts to support your side, doubling the fees. Or you could let the judge, who is not an expert in these fields, make the final decision. When you look at it that way, bringing experts to Mediation might be worth the price.

Session Schedule

The number and length of Mediation sessions can vary. Two approaches are common. The mediator will choose one based on his or her preferences and your needs.

The mediator may prefer to schedule weekly Mediation sessions of one to two hours each. This approach is customary for mediations without attorneys present. Each session focuses on a specific topic, such as child custody. The goal is to reach agreement on that issue by the end of the session. However, if agreement is not reached, the discussion can be continued the next time. The mediator may give homework to complete between sessions, such as gathering financial information or a child's medical records.

The other approach is to complete Mediation in one long session. This is the prevalent method when both spouses bring their attorneys. The goal is to settle all of the issues by the end of the day, whether that means 3:00 in the afternoon or Midnight. While the single session can be exhausting, many attorneys and clients like to bring finality to the case once and for all.

As mediators, we have tried using short sessions and long sessions; we see the benefits of both. However, most of the time we use one long session and get the matters settled in one day.

Meeting Jointly or Separately

During Mediation, you and your spouse may be seated in the same room (joint meeting) or in separate rooms (caucusing). In a joint meeting, the mediator will work with you and your spouse at the same time. With caucusing, the mediator will go from room to room, taking information and offers back and forth until an agreement is reached.

The mediator will have a preference for one method over the other. However, the strategy can be changed when needed. For example, a mediator who is using joint meetings may at times ask for a caucus to discuss a touchy topic or allow tempers to cool. If your communication styles are making joint meetings difficult, the mediator may switch to caucusing for the remainder of Mediation.

If you and your spouse are in separate rooms, get used to waiting while the mediator is discussing matters with your spouse. Do not overanalyze the amount of time the mediator spends in the other room. People communicate differently, and some take longer to get their point across than others. Be patient.

Opening Statements

Whether you meet in weekly sessions or one long session, in the same room or separate rooms, Mediation follows a similar pattern. The mediator will begin by explaining the overall goal: to reach agreement on the issues and put your agreements in writing. You will be informed of the mediator's role, the process that will be used, the ground rules that you'll follow, and the confidential nature of the proceedings. Confidentiality means, among other things, that if you and your spouse eventually go to court because you couldn't reach a mediated settlement, what was said during Mediation may not be used in the court trial. The mediator cannot be called as a witness in a hearing to explain what happened, what people said in the sessions, or why the case did not settle.

Next, the mediator will ask you and your spouse—or your attorneys, if you brought them—to make opening statements about the facts and issues involved with your case. If you haven't employed an attorney, don't think you have to give the mediator a pre-drafted statement. It's not necessary. This is simply a time for you to explain your goals for Mediation, state your views on the issues, ask any questions you may have about the process, and bring up anything else you need or want to discuss. Your statement also gives the mediator a flavor of the emotional issues that may arise during the process.

From your opening statements, the mediator will gather a substantial amount of information about the issues that need to be resolved. Usually the mediator will put the issues down on paper or on a whiteboard. This list will become the cornerstone and focus of your discussions.

Negotiation

Once the issues are defined, negotiation begins. For example, let's say you're focusing on the division of marital property. The mediator might start by gathering information about the property. Do you have a spreadsheet listing what you own and its value? If so, is all the property included? Do either of you already have an idea of how to divide the property? If you and your spouse are in separate rooms, the mediator will go from room to room, taking information and offers back and forth. If you are all in the same room, the mediator will facilitate your discussion. Either way the mediator will help you generate options for addressing specific issues and will work to reach a consensus.

The process will go on in this fashion, either in a single session or weekly sessions, until you have addressed all the issues. As agreements are reached, the mediator will informally put them down on paper in preparation for the final agreement. We suggest you take notes about what was agreed to as well.

The goal is to reach an agreement on all the issues you are confronted with. However, it's possible you will reach agreement on some of the issues and not others. For example, you might settle the issues regarding the kids, but not have enough information to settle the property issues. You can always come back to Mediation to resolve the remaining issues, if needed.

Final Agreement

At the conclusion of Mediation, the mediator will draft a final written agreement. If the mediator is not an attorney, the agreement may be called a Letter of Understanding. If the mediator is an attorney, he or she may draft either a Mediated Settlement Agreement or, in some cases, the Final Decree/Order that a judge will later sign.

The Final Agreement is crucial to the process. Once it is signed, it is binding on not only you and your spouse, but also the court that grants the divorce. So before you sign the agreement, read it carefully. Refer to your notes about what you and your spouse decided on during mediation. Make sure the final document is complete, accurate, and clear.

If you did not have an attorney representing you during Mediation, hire one to review the agreement before you sign it. Ask the attorney to review its legal implications. If the attorney raises any issues, you can return to Mediation to resolve them.

If your Mediation took place in a single, long session with attorneys present, you may feel pressure to sign the Final Agreement. It may be getting late, and everyone wants to finish up and go home. Unless you are absolutely certain about the agreement, you shouldn't sign it. This is your one chance to get the issues resolved once and for all.

If an issue arises after both of you have signed the agreement, usually the only way it can be addressed is through another Mediation. Courts cannot add to or subtract from a Mediated Settlement Agreement because in most states the court is bound by the terms of the agreement. If it's not in the agreement, then it didn't happen. If the couple reached agreements on only some of their divorce issues, the court would be bound to honor those agreements, but would then be left to decide the remaining issues.

Finalizing the Divorce

Even after you have signed the Final Agreement, you are still not divorced. A judge will need to sign a Final Decree/ Order that includes every detail of the agreement. See Chapter 16 for more information.

Mediator's Perspective
Do You Even Know What the Fight is About?

The biggest problem with Mediation is that some couples don't try it soon enough. Here's an example.

A couple who came to see me had filed for divorce 18 months earlier. Since then, each spouse had spent $35,000 on attorney fees. Yet they were no closer to resolving their issues than the day the wife had filed for divorce. The court finally ordered them to Mediation.

Both parties told me there was no way they were going to settle; something I hear almost every day. I told them they were wrong and started to figure out what, exactly, they were fighting over.

One of the issues was how much time they would each get to spend with their two kids, ages 11 and 15. Mom wanted to be awarded more time with them because Dad had cheated on her. Dad had spent his spare time with his girlfriend instead of his kids, so why should he see them as much as Mom after the divorce? Anger and stubbornness kept these two from reaching a compromise.

Neither of their attorneys brought to their attention the actual amount of time that was being disputed. It turned out the parents were arguing (and paying their lawyers to argue) over a difference of 72 hours per year. That's right, 72 hours a year—three days! When I pointed this out, they finally realized how ridiculous it was to fight. We were able to negotiate a proposal that satisfied them both.

(Continued)

They had similar problems dividing their assets. Mom wanted more than half of the assets, while Dad wanted a 50-50 split. They both had valid arguments for court, but when all was said and done, they were fighting over a difference of $10,000.

Remember, they had already spent $70,000 on attorney fees. Now their attorneys were quoting each of them $10,000 for a retainer in preparation for trial. They were spending more money on their divorce than it was worth!

What if this couple had gone to voluntary Mediation in the beginning instead of court-ordered Mediation near the end? They would have saved a tremendous amount of time, money, and emotional turmoil. Mediation works. I am certain these people wish they had tried it sooner.

I found out later that they put their divorce decree in a drawer and continued to work together to resolve other issues about their kids. I am convinced that if they hadn't gone to Mediation, they wouldn't be where they are to-day—cooperating in the best interests of their children.

Summing Up

Mediation has been hugely successful in resolving all types of disputes. What seems to be the biggest question when it comes to Mediation is *when*. Remember Mediation is not "one and done." You can employ Mediation multiple times if necessary. Try it without lawyers now and with lawyers later, or any other combination. Mediate early and see what happens. At the very least you can figure out what the issues are and come up with a plan to get them resolved.

Choosing a mediator is as important as choosing a lawyer. The right mediator for your case can make all the difference in whether you can resolve your case or not. Do your research.

If you choose Mediation, make sure you are committed to resolution, not winning. All you can expect from Mediation, or any other ADR method, is to walk away with a fair deal. In a divorce there are no winners. Appendix D provides more details on Mediation. Appendix K provides a Sample Mediated Settlement Agreement.

Mediation

A process in which a trained family law mediator, acting as a neutral third party, helps a divorcing couple reach an agreement.

Pluses

- Mediator's skills and experience are useful in resolving disputes.

- Spouses choose the mediator instead of being randomly assigned a judge in public court.

- Flexible process—can be done in one session or several, with spouses in the same room or separate rooms.

- Private way to reach agreement rather than addressing issues in a public courtroom.

(Continued)

- Faster resolution than going to court.

- Less costly than going to court.

- Offers the option of being represented by an attorney.

- Spouses maintain control over the outcome.

- Techniques learned in private mediation can be used to resolve post-divorce disputes.

Minuses

- More costly than the IHOP method.

- Like other ADR methods, doesn't work unless spouses are willing to cooperate and follow the process.

8

Collaborative Law

For every failure, there's an alternative course of action. You just have to find it. When you come to a roadblock, take a detour.

Mary Kay Ash

Perhaps your divorce issues seem too complicated for IHOP or Mediation. Or maybe you tried those methods but felt you were in over your head. If you prefer to have a lawyer represent you during the divorce process and you also understand that litigation has both financial and emotional costs, Collaborative Law might be the answer.

How Collaborative Law Works

The Collaborative Law process combines the premise of other ADR methods with full representation by an attorney. Each spouse hires a lawyer to represent his or her interests. However, Collaborative Law does not pit the two sides against each other as litigation does. Instead, everyone is on the same team. Both spouses and both attorneys work together to reach a mutually satisfying settlement of the issues surrounding the divorce. The lawyers are specially trained for this collaborative approach.

During the Collaborative Law process, as in Mediation, other professionals may be brought in to help. They might include a financial or tax specialist, a mental health professional, a pediatric behavioral specialist, or another professional needed to address a specific situation. These experts become part of the team and participate in the sessions to help resolve specific issues. The couple shares the cost of the experts and the information they provide.

In most cases, Collaborative Law is started at the beginning of the divorce process. However, if a couple tries the IHOP method or Mediation first and decides it is not the best approach, Collaborative Law is still a possibility.

Negotiating without a Mediator

When deciding whether to use Collaborative Law, couples often want to know how this process differs from Mediation. The most obvious difference is Mediation is guided by a neutral party—the mediator. This professional plays an integral role in gathering information, narrowing the issues, proposing creative solutions, and achieving agreement.

In Collaborative Law, there is no neutral third party guiding the process. The tasks that a mediator would have done are taken on by the spouses themselves, with help and guidance from their attorneys and the experts they consult. Although some couples may prefer having a mediator, the Collaborative Law approach helps couples learn to communicate with each other and work through their disagreements on their own—skills that are beneficial in the long run.

No Court Intervention

Another difference between Mediation and Collaborative Law comes into play if the spouses aren't able to settle their issues. Suppose a couple brings attorneys to their mediation sessions. If the attempt at Mediation is not successful and the couple decides to go to court, the attorneys can stay in the case and continue to represent their clients.

Collaborative Law does not allow this possibility. By entering into a Collaborative Law Agreement, the spouses and their attorneys make a commitment to avoid litigation. Court cannot be used as a threat when things get tough. If anyone on the team—spouse or attorney—attempts to go to court, the Collaborative Law process ends immediately. Both lawyers are required to withdraw from the case, and the spouses are referred to litigation attorneys.

Why wield this hammer? One reason is it gives the attorneys an incentive to stick with the Collaborative Law process even through the most difficult issues. They have no reason to talk their clients into prolonging the process (and paying more attorney fees) by going to court. In addition, the spouses are motivated to stay committed to the low-conflict way of resolving their divorce. If they sign up for Collaborative Law and cannot reach an agreement, all the time, effort, and attorney fees they have expended are wasted. This is a powerful reason to stay the course and keep working toward a solution.

Cost Considerations

Collaborative Law almost always costs less than going to court. That said, we have seen some very expensive Collaborative Law cases. To keep the costs from becoming excessive, the process must be managed well, expectations must remain realistic, and the goal of all participants must remain true.

Even so, Collaborative Law is more expensive than Mediation. For every session, you and your spouse are paying two lawyers. While the same is true if you bring lawyers to Mediation, Collaborative Law is usually a slower, more methodical process. More attorney hours means a higher legal bill.

The restrictions against going to court add a risk of even higher costs. If you and your spouse can't agree on a solution, you will both have to hire new lawyers and start over. Needless to say, this can be very expensive. The key to avoiding this outcome, as you will see, is to be honest with your attorneys from the beginning so they can properly evaluate your case for collaborative law.

Finding Attorneys

If you are considering Collaborative Law, look for attorneys who have specific training and experience in this approach. For help with hiring attorneys, read Chapter 15 and visit www.divorceinpeace.com. Before committing to the process, you and your spouse should each meet privately with your own lawyer. Discuss your goals, aspirations, needs, and concerns. Don't sugarcoat your situation. Talk about the issues and challenges of your case and any reasons it may be difficult to settle. Your attorney will evaluate your case and tell you whether Collaborative Law is likely to be successful.

Participation Agreement

If you decide to go ahead with Collaborative Law, you, your spouse, and your attorneys will then sign a Participation Agreement. This document outlines the Collaborative Law process and the mutual obligations of everyone involved. A sample is shown in Appendix J. Among other things, the agreement typically states that you and your spouse will:

- Exchange complete and accurate information about your finances and children.
- Avoid discussing divorce issues with your children or involving them in your disputes.
- Maintain absolute confidentiality during the entire process. This allows both you and your spouse to feel comfortable expressing your concerns and needs. If the case does ultimately go to trial, nothing that was said during the collaborative process can be used in court unless both of you agree.
- Bring in neutral experts as needed. These experts cannot be called to testify against either spouse if the case ultimately goes to trial.
- Authorize the attorneys to use the final written settlement agreement to obtain a Final Decree/Order.

The agreement also addresses how and when the attorneys will be paid. Be sure you understand the fees that will be involved.

The Collaborative Process

Once you have signed the Participation Agreement, you, your spouse, and your attorneys will meet in multiple sessions to reach a settlement. These sessions can last from one to four hours.

A topic for each session is usually selected in advance. These topics—which typically include property division, visitation schedules, child support, spousal support, and any other issues that need to be resolved—are discussed openly in the sessions with the goal of reaching agreement.

During your discussions, you have the benefit of the training, skills, advice, and support of your attorneys and the other professionals you bring in. You can also benefit by following the ground rules discussed in Chapter 6. They are designed to help you and your spouse communicate in a respectful, productive way and find creative solutions.

At the end of each session, the team writes down what has been agreed to and sets a game plan for the next session. You, your spouse, and the experts may be given homework assignments, such as gathering information to bring the next time.

Finalizing the Divorce

When the process is complete, the attorneys will compile the agreements from each session into a Final Decree/Order. Be sure you read this document carefully before signing it. Make sure it accurately reflects everything you agreed to during the sessions.

After you and your spouse sign the decree, you do not need to go to court to finalize your divorce. Your attorneys will file the required paperwork for you. A judge will sign the Final Decree/Order, making your divorce official.

Mediator's Perspective
Finding the Right Solution

In addition to being a mediator I have had the opportunity to represent clients as an attorney. And because I feel so strongly in the Alternative Dispute Resolution methods described in this book, I take a lot of time with each of my clients to find the ADR process best suited for their specific situation. Collaborative Law is a very viable option for many of my clients.

One client's situation comes to mind when I looked for a success story for Collaborative Law. Steve and his wife, Michelle, were married for over 14 years. They had two kids, one with a learning disability. They owned a family business, which both of them worked in. Depending on which one was valuing the business, their net worth was between $900,000 and $1.6 million.

Steve and Michelle were not overly upset with each other, but emotions were high. Steve had an affair, which obviously made Michelle angry. When Michelle first visited my office she had only known about the affair for a couple of days. She was scared, hurt, embarrassed and fearful of how the divorce would affect her kids. She was ready to file for divorce and get into court. She had a type-A personality, so she just wanted to get the divorce done and over with.

As I do with all my clients, and what your lawyer should do for you, I went over all of her options, tried to calm her down as much as possible and explained the divorce process.

(Continued)

She was too angry to consider IHOP. The affair had hurt her so much, she should couldn't stand to even look at Steve. Sitting down talking civilly to him was not an option.

Mediation was a good idea. She knew that Steve would also be consulting with an attorney in the next couple of days. Once we knew who the attorney was, I could call him or her and try to set up an early mediation. However, I explained that there will be issues with the child with a learning disability. Issues would involve education, therapies, tutors and coming up with an overall treatment plan. Steve and Michelle had often disagreed on these issues. I explained that if the case ended up in court we would have to hire an expert in learning disabilities who could testify about what the child's needs were going to be moving forward. In response, Steve would likely hire an expert to testify about these same issues but whose conclusions would be different then our experts. Ultimately, if we could not agree, a judge would have to decide.

The family business would also be another big issue. Michelle thought that the business was worth a couple of million dollars. Steve had mentioned to her that the business was tanking and was worth less than a million. Like the educational issues for the child, Steve and Michelle would each have to hire a business valuator to decide how much the business was worth. Michelle would find an expert to say that the business was worth $2 million and Steve would hire one to testify that it was worth less than a million. If they could not reach an agreement on their own, they would have to go to court and let a judge make the determination as to the value of the business.

(Continued)

Mediation would certainly be an avenue to resolve these issues, but the contested issues would cause us to have to spend a lot of money on different experts. It could work but I thought I needed to explain Collaborative Law.

I explained the "team approach" that is the cornerstone of Collaborative Law. Steve and Michelle would both be represented by lawyers, but instead of the approach associated with other ADR methods, Collaborative Law was more of a team-based solution. Everyone on the team would try to reach an agreement that would be the best for all involved. The team, the lawyers, the clients and the professionals, would all tackle the problems rather than tackling or attacking each other; instead of hiring two educational experts and two business valuators, we would hire one of each. These experts would be part of our team and would help advise us of solutions to the issues in the divorce.

But Collaborative Law does have a significant disadvantage, which I explained to Michelle. If we could not reach an agreement and the case was headed to court, I would have to withdraw from the case and she would have to start over with another lawyer, so would Steve. While this was a significant downside, I advised it was a good option so long as Steve and his lawyer would agree.

Ultimately Steve did hire a lawyer who knew the value of Collaborative Law. We all participated in the process and were able to resolve all of the issues. Collaborative Law was a success.

Collaborative Law is a very viable option for those going through a divorce. It can become expensive like any

> **(Continued)**
>
> other process, but had we not been able to resolve the issues and had to go to court, it would have been much more expensive. It takes the right lawyers and the right clients to make Collaborative Law a success.
>
> Find the right lawyer who knows and has experience in collaborative law and you are half way there.

Summing Up

Collaborative Law shares many of the advantages of other ADR methods. It is less costly, more private, and more flexible than going to court. It gives control of the process to the spouses, not a judge. It reduces conflict, promotes cooperation, and minimizes the emotional effects of divorce on the spouses and children. Collaborative Law empowers couples to dissolve their marriage with dignity.

Compared to the other ADR methods discussed so far, Collaborative Law has many similarities and some significant differences. It is more expensive than the IHOP method or Mediation. Like IHOP, it follows the philosophy that couples are capable of resolving their own issues. At the same time, it provides the legal representation that IHOP is missing. Unlike Mediation, Collaborative Law does not include a neutral facilitator, but it does provide for specially trained legal counsel.

Collaborative Law can be advantageous for certain couples. Among them are those with especially complicated issues regarding finances or children, requiring the support of attorneys and other professionals. If there are significant power imbalances in the relationship, then Collaborative Law is often a better choice than IHOP or Mediation. For many couples, Collaborative Law is a good option that should be considered in pursuit of a Divorce in Peace. Appendix E provides greater details regarding Collaborative Law.

Collaborative Law

An Alternative Dispute Resolution process in which the spouses, their attorneys, and appropriate professionals work together in good faith to resolve divorce issues without court intervention.

Pluses

- Includes full representation by an attorney for each spouse.

- Minimizes conflict; encourages teamwork and cooperation.

- Less costly than going to court.

- Gives attorneys and spouses a financial incentive for not going to court.

- Private way to reach agreement rather than addressing issues in a public courtroom.

- Spouses maintain control over the outcome.

(Continued)

- Allows flexibility and creative solutions.

- Advantageous in cases with complicated issues or power imbalances.

Minuses

- No mediator to act as a neutral party.

- Costs more than IHOP method and mediation.

- Takes longer than IHOP and mediation.

- Like other ADR methods, doesn't work unless spouses are willing cooperate, share financial information candidly, and follow the process.

9

Arbitration

At all events, arbitration is more rational, just,
and humane than the resort to the sword.
Richard Cobden

What happens in high-conflict cases where you absolutely need
a judge to make decisions regarding your divorce, but you want
to avoid the time and expense of a court trial? An alternative
to the use of the public court system is hiring an arbitrator, or
private judge to hear evidence and decide your case.

What Is Arbitration?

Arbitration is a dispute resolution process through which
conflicts are decided by a neutral third party, called an arbitrator or private judge. Arbitrators are usually retired judges
or highly qualified lawyers who have a reputation of being
knowledgeable and fair. Unlike a court trial, which also
involves a judge, Arbitration takes place outside the public
judicial system, usually in a law office.

During Arbitration, each spouse is represented by an attorney. Unlike Collaborative Law, in which spouses and attorneys all work together, Arbitration is an adversarial process. "Adversarial" does not mean you and your spouse are required to get angry and yell at each other—and we certainly hope you don't. It simply means there are two sides to the case, just as in a court trial. Both sides want the issues surrounding the divorce, such as property division and child custody, to be settled in their favor.

Arbitration typically takes several months. In a series of hearings, the attorneys make their respective cases by presenting evidence to the arbitrator. At the final hearing, the arbitrator decides the case.

Divorcing couples are never ordered to go to arbitration; unlike mediation, which is sometimes ordered by the court. If you want to use Arbitration, you must elect to do so on your own. You might choose this method at the beginning of your divorce if you are convinced other methods will not be successful. Or you can try other methods first, then use Arbitration to settle any issues that remain unresolved.

Why Not Just Go to Court?

You can already see how Arbitration is different from the other ADR methods described in this book. It's adversarial rather than cooperative, and the couple has no control over the final decision. So why not just have a trial in court? Actually, Arbitration offers many advantages over a court trial.

Choice of arbitrator. In the court system, you have no input as to who will be deciding your case. In Arbitration, you and your spouse choose the arbitrator. You'll read more about how to do this later in the chapter.

Privacy. In a court trial, your dirty laundry is hung out for all to see. Every argument, every innuendo, every accusation is discussed in an open forum—the courtroom. All of the evidence and transcripts are public records viewable by anyone. Arbitration, in contrast, is conducted outside the public forum, typically in the office of the arbitrator. The filings, evidence, and decisions are private. Any paperwork filed with the arbitrator is kept in the arbitrator's office opposed to an open governmental file.

Less formality and stress. Courtrooms can be intimidating. Since Arbitration takes place in a law office, the hearings typically feel less formal, and because you have more privacy, you are likely to feel less stressed.

Easier access, fewer delays. One of the most frustrating aspects of the court system is delays are inevitable. The system is simply too overcrowded to keep up. A judge may have 40 cases on his or her docket. Most judges take the shortest case first, then work their way down the list. As a result, it is not at all unusual to wait for hours to appear before the judge. Meanwhile, you are missing work and paying lawyers to sit there and do nothing. Or you may show up on a Monday and be told to come back later in the week or, in the worst case, months later. The cost of an attorney preparing for the same hearing multiple times is enormous. With Arbitration, you shouldn't run into these situations. Your "judge" (the arbitrator) is at your disposal. When the arbitrator sets your case for a hearing, he or she will, or at least should, be on time. In addition, the arbitrator is "on call"—generally available on short notice to resolve issues. If a dispute arises, all you and your spouse usually have to do is make a conference call to the arbitrator and talk through the issues.

Less expensive. Arbitration certainly has its costs. In contrast to a divorce trial, in which the state pays for the judge, you and your spouse must pay the arbitrator. However, this cost is offset by the savings you gain because of fewer delays. You will see later the discovery process is more efficient and less costly in Arbitration than in a court trial.

Hiring an Arbitrator

Hiring an arbitrator is an important decision. Remember, the arbitrator is going to decide all issues involved in your case. You and your spouse must agree on who this person will be.

Probably the most persuasive credential a family law arbitrator could have is experience as a former judge who has presided over family law cases. Former judges are likely to be well known in the area where they presided. Therefore, the best search strategy is to ask local attorneys for a recommendation. If they name a candidate, inquire about the person's qualities while a judge or as an arbitrator. You might ask whether the person has an appropriate judicial temperament, makes reasoned and impartial decisions, is well versed in property division and child custody issues, and will get the case concluded in an efficient manner.

Next, do additional research on the arbitrators that were recommended. Look up appellate court cases they were involved in as judges. Determine what issues were appealed and the result of each appeal. Review arbitrators' résumés as well. These can often be found on websites, or you can call to request them. Look for how many years of experience each person has as an arbitrator and a court judge. Also find out what you can about their experience as attorneys—the law firms they worked for, the types of cases they handled, and whether they tended to represent husbands or wives.

Once you narrow down the list of possible arbitrators, you will want to interview them. During the interview, it isn't appropriate to ask how the person feels about a particular issue in your case, nor to provide a factual scenario and ask who should win. You are simply trying to determine whether the candidate has the requisite qualifications, temperament, and experience necessary to decide the issues in your case. You will also want to ask questions about the process, such as: How much do you charge? About how long will the process take? What's your availability when it comes to scheduling hearings? If we have a dispute, can we call you and get it resolved over the phone?

Once you hire an arbitrator, you must live with your choice. As soon as the case starts, the arbitrator will start making decisions. If the decisions don't go the way you'd like, you can't say, "Oops, I made a mistake. I want to find another arbitrator." That would conflict with the entire purpose of Arbitration, which is to get a fair, efficient resolution to your dispute.

Binding or Nonbinding Arbitration

Before you agree to Arbitration, you and your spouse must decide whether it will be binding or nonbinding. If it is binding, the arbitrator's decision is final and cannot be appealed. If it is nonbinding and one spouse does not like the decision, the case ends up going to court.

We recommend Binding Arbitration. What is the point in going to Arbitration if it is not binding? Whatever the decision, you want it to be final so this chapter in your life can be closed. You want to avoid the time, expense, and emotional cost of appeals. If for some reason you prefer Non-binding Arbitration, you are better off going to court now instead of going through the exercise of an arbitration that won't stick.

It's worth noting that if you go to court and you think the judge got it wrong, you can appeal the decision to a higher court. However, appeals on family law cases are rarely successful. So the inability to appeal a binding arbitration is not really as much of a disadvantage as you might think.

Getting Started

As previously mentioned, you and your spouse will each need your own attorney. Any divorce lawyer is qualified to represent clients in Arbitration. Review the guidelines for hiring an attorney in Chapter 15.

Before beginning the process, you, your spouse, and your attorneys will sign an Arbitration Agreement. This document spells out the terms of the arbitration, such as whether it will be binding or nonbinding. As always, read the agreement carefully and make sure you understand it before signing.

The arbitrator will need some preliminary information about the facts of your case. This may be provided at an initial meeting between the arbitrator and the attorneys. You and your spouse might attend this meeting as well. Some arbitrators simply ask the attorneys to provide a written explanation.

After the initial information has been provided, the arbitration hearings begin. Most of them have to do with sharing documents through the discovery process.

Limited Discovery

As you may recall from Chapter 3, Discovery is the process of requesting and obtaining information during a legal proceeding. In a court case, Discovery is governed by the rules of civil procedure. These rules limit the number of certain types of requests, but others are unlimited. For example, one spouse could serve the other with 500 requests to produce specific financial documents. A great deal of time can be spent objecting to requests, answering requests, disagreeing over whether they were answered adequately, and so on. Of course, whenever you're dealing with courts and attorneys, time is money. Discovery accounts for most of the cost of litigation.

In Arbitration, the rules regarding Discovery are set by the arbitrator. Compared to a judge in a court trial, the arbitrator has a better handle on the spouses' financial resources and can use this knowledge to determine the best use of Discovery in that particular case. The arbitrator can limit the number of requests and the time spent on depositions and interrogatories. These limitations can be adjusted as the case proceeds. The arbitrator can decide which requests are relevant to the case and which are not. Unlike a judge, an arbitrator is allowed to make a decision based on incomplete evidence if the available evidence is deemed conclusive. If there is a discovery dispute, the arbitrator can easily get on the phone with the lawyers to discuss it. All of these factors help save time and money.

Outside Experts

To help resolve specific issues, outside experts, such as accountants or child behavior specialists, can be brought in. Since Arbitration is an adversarial process, both sides hire and pay their own experts. For example, if the couple owns a small business, one spouse's expert could testify it is worth x dollars. In response, the other side could hire a qualified expert to testify that the business is worth only y dollars. The arbitrator would ultimately decide.

In some circumstances, the arbitrator can appoint one

expert to provide information that will help the arbitrator make a decision. The initial cost of this expert is usually allocated equally between the spouses. The arbitrator has the ability to reallocate the expenses later, if a different division seems appropriate.

Final Decision

At the end of the process, the arbitrator prepares a document called an Arbitrator's Award or Arbitrator's Decision. This document should outline all decisions made by the arbitrator, but is not required to explain the reasoning behind them. As noted earlier, if you are using binding arbitration, the decision is final and cannot be appealed.

Based on that decision, the attorneys prepare a Final Decree/Order and present it to the arbitrator for signature. If there are disagreements about the wording of the final decree, they are decided by the arbitrator. The Final Decree will then be provided to a judge for his or her signature, making the divorce official.

Combined Mediation/Arbitration

Before we leave the topic of arbitration, you may want to consider another option. You can choose a process that combines the concepts of Mediation and Arbitration. It is called Mediation/Arbitration; "med/arb" or "med-arb." The neutral third-party first acts as a mediator, using the procedures and techniques discussed in Chapter 7. The couple works together, with the mediator's help, to resolve as many issues as they can. If they reach full agreement, the process ends there. Otherwise, if some disputes remain unresolved and efforts to mediate the case have been exhausted, the mediator becomes an arbitrator and decides the remaining issues. If this approach interests you, ask your attorney or prospective arbitrators about mediation/arbitration.

This process can be very effective. It allows the party to work hard on resolving their issues themselves with the assistance of the mediator. So the process has all the benefits of Mediation. Unlike Mediation, the issues that cannot be resolved are submitted to the arbitrator to decide. This enables the couple to avoid court, maintain privacy and have some finality to their divorce. Without the Arbitration, as we learned in Chapter 7 on Mediation, the unresolved issues would have to be litigated in front of a judge. The judge would have to hear a lot more about all of the issues to make a fair decision. The arbitrator already knows the case, the issues and how those issues have been resolved. That puts the arbitrator in a unique position to quickly make decisions about the remaining issues.

Judge's Perspective
Putting Your Life Story on Stage

Courtrooms are open to the public. Anyone who wants to come and watch a case on trial is allowed. In fact, not even the judge can close the courtroom if he wants. I have certainly wanted to close the courtroom a time or two. Not for my own sake, but for the sake of those who were in my court talking about extremely personal matters.

I had a divorce case in which the dad was addicted to pornography and the mom was addicted to meth. As a result of their addictions the facts against both of them were horrendous. Dad had hired prostitutes, had strangers over to the house and had spent a considerable amount of money to support his porn addiction.

Mom had hit rock bottom. She looked awful. She had basically abandoned the family and was sleeping on people's couches. She had likewise spent a lot of money supporting her drug habit.

All of the problems the family faced were now being discussed in public. Mom and Dad were both called as witnesses where they had to answer for all their indiscretions, crossed examined by the other spouse's attorney which was more of an effort to embarrass them than helping me make a decision about what to do with their kids and finances.

Although the majority of the public couldn't care less about this family and their problems, the public also includes their friends and family. While they were there to support their family member or friends, they also had a front row seat to the good, the bad and the ugly. I could not imagine myself having to answer the most personal questions about my life in front of my friends, family or the family of my soon-to-be-ex.

While I hope you do not have the severity of problems this couple had, there are certainly private matters in your life that you do not want to discuss in front of your family and friends, much less strangers.

Arbitration allows you to have your day in court in front of an arbitrator that you choose. You and your attorney can air all of your grievances you have against your spouse, and your spouse has the same opportunity. In the end, a judge/arbitrator will make a decision. The primary

(Continued)

difference is this will all play out in the privacy of a law office and not in court. The arbitrator can also exclude anyone and everyone from the process and ensure that any of the paperwork filed in the case is not open to the public. The only downside to Arbitration is that the arbitrator's decision is not generally subject to appeal. But in all honesty, most family law appeals do not change a court's decision.

Summing Up

If you cannot otherwise resolve your divorce disputes, then seriously look at Arbitration. You have already given up control of the result of your case because you could not settle. Compared to a court trial, Arbitration speeds up the divorce process, saves money, and provides complete privacy. Arbitration is not commonly used in the family law/divorce context, so not many lawyers will recommend it. But take the initiative to have a full and complete discussion about Arbitration with your attorney. Weighing the pros and the cons might lead you to choose Arbitration as a method of resolving your divorce.

If you like Arbitration, but would like the opportunity to resolve whatever issues you can with your spouse, then look into Mediation/Arbitration; "med/arb" or "med-arb." It can be a very useful tool in resolving your divorce. Appendix F provides greater details surrounding Arbitration. Appendix L provides a Binding Arbitration Sample Agreement.

Arbitration

A voluntary process outside the judicial system that involves hiring a neutral third party, called an arbitrator or private judge, to hear evidence and make final decisions in a divorce case.

Pluses

- Spouses choose arbitrator (rather than being randomly assigned a judge in public court)

- Private process; information is confidential

- More informal and less stressful than court trial

- Takes less time than court trial

- Generally less expensive than court trial

- Appropriate for high-conflict cases

Minuses

- Adversarial rather than cooperative

- Spouses pay for arbitrator and other case expenses

- Costs more than IHOP, mediation, and collaborative law

- Spouses don't control the outcome

Part Three

Negotiating the Issues

10

Assets and Debts

Whoever said "Marriage is a 50-50 proposition" laid the foundation for more divorce fees than any other short sentence in our language.

Austin Elliot

Standup comedians have often used divorce as a subject of their jokes. The punch line is usually some extreme example of how their ex-spouse connived with a shady lawyer to get the house, the car, and most of the money.

There's a grain of truth behind these jokes. Many divorcing couples feel it necessary to fight over who will win a bigger piece of the pie. Yet in reality, if they take the battle to court, neither of them may get what they want. Alternative Dispute Resolution offers couples more control for working out property division in a way that both spouses will agree with.

How a Judge Would Divide Property

If you were getting your divorce through a court trial, the judge would divide your assets and debts for you. State divorce laws affect the way a judge would divide assets and debts. A key factor is whether you live in a Community Property State or an Equitable Distribution State.

When you use ADR methods, you and your spouse have more freedom to divide your assets and debts in any way you choose, as long as you come to a mutual agreement. However, it's still helpful to know what decision a judge would most likely make. This information gives you a realistic starting point for your negotiations. You and your spouse can save time by not making unreasonable demands. And just in case you end up taking your divorce to court, you'll have an idea of what to expect from the judge.

Community Property States

In Community Property States, all assets acquired during the marriage are considered to be community property. That means the property belongs to both spouses equally, no matter which spouse acquired the item, whose name is on it, or whose income paid for it. In a divorce, each spouse is presumed to own half of the community property. In legal terms, this is called "undivided one-half interest."

Similarly, all debts acquired during the marriage are community debts. Each spouse has one-half of the responsibility for that debt, no matter who incurred it.

Any property or debts acquired before the marriage are separate property. In addition, any inheritance received, even during the marriage, is the separate property of the person who inherited the money. The court cannot take separate property from one spouse and give it to the other.

As of this writing, there are nine Community Property States: Arizona, California, Idaho, Louisiana, Nevada, New Mexico, Texas, Washington, and Wisconsin. Couples living in Alaska have the option to "opt in" for community property. Puerto Rico is a Community Property Jurisdiction.

Equitable Distribution States

All other states and territories not listed above are Equitable Distribution States. In these states, all property acquired during the marriage belongs to the spouse who earned or purchased it. However, at the time of divorce, the property would be divided in a fair and equitable manner. There are not any specific rules or formulas to determine how much of the property each spouse will receive. The court would look at a variety of factors to make a determination as to what a fair and equitable division of the property would be.

In Equitable Distribution States, just as in Community Property States, some assets are off limits when the court divides the property. Inheritances are separate property, whether they were received before or during the marriage. Assets acquired before the marriage are also considered to be separate property, unless the ownership has changed in the meantime.

Fault

When settling a divorce, judges may also consider the issue of Fault. If it can be proven that one spouse is at fault for the divorce, the other spouse may get more of the marital assets. Fault usually refers to marital misconduct. Grounds for fault can be adultery, drug use, abandonment, abuse of the spouse or a child, or cruelty, to name a few. In many states, mental illness or mental incompetence is also considered grounds for Fault, even though it does not involve intentional wrongdoing.

All states allow some form of No-Fault divorce. Under these rules, it is not necessary for one spouse to prove that the other is at fault. The grounds for divorce would be Irreconcilable Differences or Conflict of Personalities. However, even in a No-Fault divorce, there are many instances in which a judge may takes facts about who "caused" the divorce into consideration when dividing the property in a fair and equitable way.

From our experience, it is rare for a judge to give the non-fault party more than 60% of the marital assets. We have certainly seen cases where one spouse was awarded greater than 60% of the assets. However, in those cases the facts justifying the award were extreme. Keep this in mind when using your chosen ADR process. If you cannot settle and end up in court, the most you will likely receive is an extra 10% of the marital assets. So do not go into ADR with the notion that you are going to get 80% of the assets because your spouse is at fault. It is unrealistic. Asking for more than 50-50 is reasonable. Demanding more than 60-40, in most circumstances, is not. Approach property division in a way that is based on sound business sense rather than emotion.

Listing Assets and Debts

Now that you have an understanding of how a judge might rule and have set reasonable expectations, you and your spouse can begin the process of dividing your assets and debts using your chosen ADR method.

The first step is to identify exactly what you own and what you owe. To accomplish this, you and your spouse will need to compile a complete list of all assets and debts. In legal terms, this is called an Inventory and Appraisement (I&A). You can find a sample I&A form in Appendix M, or download a copy from our website at www.divorceinpeace.com, Helpful Links. This list of assets and debts is essential to guide you and your spouse through the division of property, item by item.

Since you're using ADR, you and your spouse can choose to work together to list your assets and debts. If you're unable to work together, each of you will make a list and give it to the other spouse.

The I&A form has two main parts. The first is for community or joint estate (also known as marital estate)—in other words, things you own together. In this context, "estate" is just another word for assets and debts. The second part is for separate estates (things each of you own separately). List each asset and debt in the appropriate section, based on when it was acquired and the laws of your state. As explained earlier, separate property generally includes assets and debts acquired before the marriage, as well as all inheritances and gifts. Assets or debts that are a mixture of separate property and marital property should be listed in both sections. If you're not sure how to list property, consult your attorney or financial advisor.

The I&A form includes sections for many specific types of assets and debts. Copy the sections as needed; for example, to show multiple bank accounts or credit cards. Fill in the specific details that the form requests, such as dates, account numbers, and value.

As you're making your list, don't worry yet about how the assets and debts will be divided. Your initial goal is simply to identify what you and your spouse own and what you owe.

Determining the Value of Property

In order to divide your assets and debts fairly, it's essential to know their monetary value. Sometimes it's difficult to determine the value, or you and your spouse may come up with different estimates. In these cases you can rely on trade publications or experts to determine the value. For example, you might use the trade publication *Kelly Blue Book* for valuing cars. To determine the value of your home, you will probably have to employ a real estate appraiser.

One of the most difficult items to determine is the value of a family business. We recommend you hire a business valuator to set a value from which negotiations can begin.

For some assets, you will need to enter two values: the value on the date of your marriage and the current value. This would be the case if, for example, you made contributions to a retirement plan before your marriage and continued to do so after your marriage. Knowing both values makes it possible to determine how much of the account balance is separate property and how much is marital property. For example, a $300,000 retirement account might have had a value of $25,000 at the time of the marriage. That roughly means $25,000 of the account is separate property and $275,000 is marital property.

Listing Claims

Certain sections of the I&A form involve claims or contingencies. You may or may not need to fill out these sections, depending on your situation.

Some claims involve money that is expected to be paid by a third party at some point. For example, suppose the wife was in a serious auto accident and filed a lawsuit against the other driver. The expected amount of the award would be listed under "Contingent Assets" (Section 27 of the sample I&A form in the Appendix). Other examples include insurance claims, unemployment claims, employment discrimination claims, and Veterans Administration claims.

Some sections of the I&A form involve claims between separate and marital estates. For instance, the separate estate of one spouse may need to reimburse the marital estate—perhaps to make up for a prior transaction in which separate property and marital property were mingled. These types of claims, and the legal wording used on the I&A form to describe them, can be complicated. You may want to ask your attorney or financial advisor for advice.

Notarizing the I&A

Both spouses should sign the I&A form in the presence of a notary, whether you prepare the I&A together or separately. Doing so signifies that the information is true and correct to the best of your knowledge, under penalty of perjury. Notarization provides reassurance that neither spouse is intentionally hiding information or being untruthful.

Nevertheless, it's possible that you may not be aware of some assets and debts that your spouse knows about, and vice versa. After the I&As have been completed, you, your spouse, and your attorneys will compare the two forms and work out any discrepancies.

Dividing the Pie

Now you and your spouse have a complete list of assets and debts and their value. What's next? If you have a prenuptial agreement then you already have a plan for how to divide your property in a divorce. Otherwise, you will need to have an educated discussion on how to divide it all.

Before you get down to allocating specific items, the two of you will need to address a fundamental question: What is a fair division? Should each spouse get 50% of the assets and 50% of the debt, or would a different proportion be fairer?

If you took your divorce to a court trial, the judge would decide on a fair property division by taking a number of factors into consideration. Depending on your situation, the same factors may play a part in your negotiations as well. Examples include:

The income and future earning capacity of each spouse. A spouse with little or no income may be given more of the marital property at the time of divorce. Why? This spouse has a greater need. The spouse with the higher income can recover from the financial woes of a divorce much more quickly.

The value of homemaking and child care provided during the marriage. During the marriage, one spouse may have given up potential income in order to take care of the home and the children. Most of us don't track the financial worth of homemaking and parenting, but they definitely have monetary value—in addition to their other benefits. It's important to take this value into account when dividing property in a divorce. The stay-at-home spouse may not have increased the couple's bank balance, but should be credited for contributing to the marital assets in other ways.

Other contributions made during the marriage. Suppose a husband decides to change careers in order to earn more money. He goes back to school to earn a degree in his new field. His wife takes an extra job to pay for his tuition. After the husband graduates, the couple decides to divorce. This means the wife will not receive the benefits of her husband's higher pay, even though she financially supported his education. The property division can be adjusted to compensate for this discrepancy.

The length of the marriage. Assume one spouse brought more assets into the marriage than the other. Property might be divided very differently depending on whether the marriage lasted 30 years or only nine months.

The age and health of the spouses. Suppose the husband is older and was recently diagnosed with a debilitating disease. The wife is younger, still healthy, and working. It would be appropriate for the husband to receive more of the assets at the time of divorce because that will be the only money he will have to survive, while the wife still can earn a living.

The standard of living established during the marriage. Depending on where you live, this factor could significantly impact the property division. It is weighed more heavily in some states than others. Do your own research or consult an attorney in your state to see how this issue might affect your negotiations.

Whether one spouse can be held at fault in the breakup of the marriage. As mentioned previously, fault may need to be considered when dividing assets and debts. It will not result in a financial windfall, but may make a difference in some cases.

Discussing these issues with your spouse can be challenging. Remember that the goal of ADR is to avoid conflict and negotiate in peace. It's a good idea to review the ground rules explained in Chapter 6. Depending on your ADR method, you can also get help from your mediator, arbitrator, or attorney. If you and your spouse have considerable separate property, it would advisable to consult an attorney before you settle your divorce.

Remember, too, that once you agree on a fair division in

principle, you must be flexible in practice. You can't divide the dining room table or the big screen TV by taking out a power saw and cutting them in half. You'll need to come up with other solutions—perhaps selling them and splitting the money, or trading one asset for another. Even financial accounts can be tricky to divide. For example, there are tax consequences for cashing out a 401(k). Throughout the negotiation process, be open to give and take. You cannot divide every single item, but you can strive to be fair.

Using a Spreadsheet

The best way to work out a property division is to use a spreadsheet. A sample is provided in Appendix R. It should have two sections, one for assets and one for debts. List all the assets or debts in the first column and their values in the second column. Label the third and fourth columns with each of your names. As you agree on who takes what, put the value of the item in the column for that spouse. The goal is for the totals in each section of the spreadsheet to match the overall division that you have agreed on. For example, if you agree that one spouse should get 65% of the assets and 45% of the debts, the spreadsheet will show whether you have achieved that goal.

What to Do with the House

Your home is often the biggest asset acquired during a marriage. It can also be one of the most complicated to deal with when dividing property.

The Emotional Side

In addition to its financial value, your home may have a strong emotional value to one or both of you. Sometimes, emotions do not represent reality. A spouse may be emotionally attached to the house, yet unable to afford it after the divorce. This is a harsh reality to face.

If you are in this situation, try to focus on the fact that the house is only a house. A home is whatever and wherever you make it. After the divorce, you will have an opportunity to make a new home and new memories. Once you understand this point, you can focus your negotiations on the financial picture.

What's It Worth?

Before deciding what to do with your home, you and your spouse must determine its value. To do this, you will need to have the property appraised. You can look for appraisers at www.divorceinpeace.com, do an Internet search, or ask your friends for recommendations. Make sure any appraisers you consider are certified; most states require that they are. They should also be experienced and familiar with your local housing market.

After you determine the appraised value, enter it on the I&A form. Also enter the amount owed on the mortgage and any other liens against the property. Subtract these amounts from the appraised value to determine the net equity. This is the value that you and your spouse will negotiate how to divide.

Because of the negative effects from refinancing, the mortgage crises, and a slump in housing values, your home may not be worth what it once was or what you hoped it would be. Keep in mind that no matter how much money you've put into the home or how much you think its worth, there is only one true way to figure out its value: put it up for sale and see what someone is willing to pay for it. If you're not ready to do that yet, the best course is to rely on your appraiser's professional judgment. This person has the knowledge and experience to make a realistic assessment based on local market conditions. Don't overestimate your home's value because of wishful thinking.

What if you find out your home is worth less than what you owe on the mortgage? In that case, you'll need to seek professional help to see what options you have. Ask your mortgage company if you can negotiate a new loan. Talk to a lawyer to see what liability you would have to the mortgage company if you sold the home for less than you owe. You might also consult a bankruptcy attorney to see if filing bankruptcy would benefit you.

Sell or Keep?

To "divide" your home, you basically have two choices: You can sell the home and split the equity, or you can agree that Spouse A will keep the home in exchange for giving Spouse B something else. Possible options include making a cash payment to Spouse B, refinancing the mortgage in Spouse A's name, or giving Spouse B a larger share of other assets.

Before making this decision, give careful consideration to whether either of you actually want to keep the house—and if you do, whether that would be a practical solution. Questions to consider include:

- Who will the kids primarily live with? How important is it for them to stay in this home?
- Can you afford to maintain the home on your own? Consider the cost of repairs, property taxes, heating and cooling, and other continuing expenses.
- Does your spouse need the equity out of the home

now? If so, do you have enough cash to pay your spouse's share of the equity?

- Is refinancing the mortgage in your own name a possibility? Could you do so within a reasonable amount of time?

The ability to exchange other assets for home equity can help bridge the gap in negotiations. For example, suppose the wife wants to keep the home, but cannot afford to pay her spouse cash for his portion of the equity. The husband wants to keep his 401(k) intact. If the wife's share of the 401(k) is similar to the husband's share of the home equity, you can start to see the middle ground for an agreement. The wife keeps the home and all of its equity, while the husband keeps his 401(k). This solution seems to make sense. It would seem equally sensible to a judge if the case went to court.

By the way, the options you and your spouse have when using ADR are the same options the court has. When many couples go to court, both spouses want to keep the home and are unable to agree on its value. Both spouses hire separate real estate experts to testify to the likely value of the home. The judge knows the only way to really determine the value of the home is to sell it. It is within the judge's power to order that the home be sold and the net equity split between the spouses. Be careful what you wish for. In cases like this, both spouses spend a lot of money on attorneys. And in the end, the judge may sell the house then neither spouse gets the house.

If You Sell

If you and your spouse do decide to sell the home, you'll need to set an asking price. It's always tempting to set the price as high as possible. If you think the home is worth more than the appraiser estimated, you can put it on the market and see what happens. If you don't get any leads, the price is probably too high. Your real estate agent can give you another perspective on the price and any other possible reasons the home is not selling. You can find real estate agents in your area at www.divorceinpeace.com.

It's usually better to set a price that will result in a quick sale. Remember the costs of keeping the house while you try to sell it: upkeep, utility bills, insurance, and property taxes. The longer the house stays on the market, the more money you have to pay to maintain it and the less money you will ultimately make on the sale.

Settling Up

No matter what you and your spouse choose to do with your home, ultimately you will need to settle up. If you sell the home, you must determine who gets what percentage of the proceeds. If one of you keeps the home, you will need to agree on what, if anything, the other spouse receives in exchange for giving up his or her share of ownership. Depending on your situation, these decisions may be fairly simple or more complex.

For example, suppose the home was purchased during the marriage and is sold during the divorce. The spouses agree that each of them is entitled to half its value. Therefore, their property division agreement states that the proceeds of the sale will be divided equally. This is about as simple as it can get.

Now consider a more complicated scenario. Let's say the wife inherited the home from her parents. An inheritance is considered separate property, so the wife is the sole owner of the home and will continue to own it after the divorce.

However, during the marriage the couple used joint funds to pay for home renovations. This may entitle the joint estate to be reimbursed for a portion of the home remodel or increased value of the home by the wife's separate estate. The couple will need to calculate the amount of the reimbursement and show it on the I&A form as a claim. In more complicated situations like this, an attorney or financial advisor can provide helpful guidance.

Personal Property

You may have seen or heard of the Hollywood movie *War of the Roses.* In it, Barbara and Oliver Rose are getting a divorce that gets way out of hand. They fight over everything. This happens in real life too. In our legal and judicial experience, we have seen clients fighting over china, garden hoses, placemats, and window treatments.

Judge's Perspective
Don't Sweat the Small Stuff

I once had a divorce case where the couple made agreements on almost all substantive issues, but could not agree on a few personal property items they both wanted. They had a trial just to settle the ownership of those items. The property included a barbecue grill, a camping tent, children's furniture, and a TV. The total value was in the neighborhood of $1,000.

(Continued)

The biggest fight was over the camping tent. They disagreed about its value and whether it was community property or separate property. I asked the spouses how much they thought it was worth. Their estimates were between $100 and $200. They must have spent well over this amount on attorney's fees for the trial. I ordered that the tent be either sold or donated to charity, with the proceeds or tax deduction to be divided equally.

Judges have many creative ways to deal with personal property. For example, I've told spouses that all disputed personal property will be placed in a pile. The husband, I explain, will flip a coin and the wife will call it in the air. The winner of the coin toss will get to choose an item from the pile, and then the other spouse will choose. This process will be repeated until all remaining personal property is disposed of. Sounds ridiculous, doesn't it? Yet this solution is no more ridiculous than people spending money fighting over personal property. When I order this type of division, what usually happens is the spouses realize how foolish they have been and reach an agreement.

Property can have sentimental value to both you and your spouse. As you move forward with your divorce, the sentiments will become more intense. You can hang on to some things, but you will have to let go of others. Try your best to make solid decisions based on reality and not emotions. Certainly some personal property items will have an emotional value, but they should be very few. In those instances, realize how much heartache and turmoil you could expend on the item. Keep it all in perspective. Property is just property. Your dignity is your dignity. Do not trade one for the other.

Dividing Debt

Dividing the pie also involves debt. Credit card debt is often the death of the family's finances. You and your spouse will have to decide how to divide the debt, including any tax liabilities. Perhaps one spouse will receive a larger share of the assets but, as a result, have to take on more of the debt. The spouse with the greater income is in a better financial position to take on debt than the person who makes less.

It is important to note that while ADR agreements or court orders can specify that one spouse will pay a certain debt, this does not change the contractual obligation with the person or institution you owe money to. For example, if both of you took out a mortgage on your home, the fact that your spouse has agreed to make the mortgage payments does not get you out of your contractual obligation to pay the debt. How should you address this? When making agreements to take over debt, it is best to agree to immediately put the debt in the responsible spouse's name. This might mean refinancing the mortgage in one spouse's name, for example, or transferring the balance of a credit card to a card solely in one spouse's name.

Finalizing the Property Division

Once you and your spouse have decided how to divide your property, you will need to spell out your decisions in a written document. This will become part of the overall written agreement that you arrive at through the IHOP method, Mediation, or Collaborative Law. If you're using Arbitration, the arbitrator will make the decisions.

The property division agreement will need to become part of your Final Decree/Order. The easiest method is to simply attach the property division to the decree. However, this method has a distinct disadvantage. When the decree is filed with the court, all of the details about your assets and debts will become part of the public record. To get around this, you can ask that the decree say there is an agreement dividing the property, but it is not attached at the request of the parties. In that instance, you and your spouse should each keep an originally signed property division agreement in your files. If you have used attorneys, they should keep copies as well.

Summing Up

Dividing your assets and debts can be an emotional and tedious process. When discussing the division of your property focus primarily on what makes financial sense rather than on emotional attachments.

Financial difficulties can cause an enormous amount of stress in the best of circumstances. Going through all of your property and debts during a divorce and realizing what will be left after the divorce will no doubt be even more stressful.

Try to approach the division of your property with as much information as possible and negotiate in a constructive way. Understand that you and your spouse being scared of your economic futures is normal, but do not let that worry and stress interfere with your ability to constructively negotiate. You now know that not settling your case will only further the financial stress you are now feeling. Court does not make financial sense, try to avoid it and settle using an ADR method.

11

Spousal Support

When two people decide to get a divorce, it isn't
a sign that they don't "understand" one other,
but a sign that they have, at last, begun to.
Helen Rowland

One of the most contentious issues that can arise during
divorce is Spousal Support, also known as Alimony or
Spousal Maintenance. Spousal Support differs from dividing
property, which was discussed in the last chapter. Property
division involves looking at what the spouses jointly own
and owe at the time of the divorce and splitting those assets
and debts between them. Spousal Support typically involves
payments given from one spouse to the other over a period
of time.

Spousal Support may be necessary at two points in the
divorce process. Temporary Spousal Support is paid before
the divorce is final. Post-Divorce Support is paid after the
divorce is final. Both types have a similar purpose: to lessen

the economic hardship that one of the spouses would otherwise experience during or after the divorce.

Temporary Spousal Support

When a couple first begins the divorce process, their home life can be quite chaotic. That includes managing their finances. Assuming the spouses move apart, suddenly there are two households to support instead of one. If one of the spouses earns considerably less than the other, the financial impact on the lesser earning spouse can be devastating.

Temporary Spousal Support is designed to reduce that immediate impact. While the divorce is pending, the higher earning spouse (paying spouse) makes payments to the lesser earning spouse (the receiving spouse). These payments recur on a regular basis, usually monthly. The payments ensure that the lesser earning spouse has sufficient cash flow to pay rent, utility bills, car payments, credit card bills, and other expenses during this time. Temporary Spousal Support begins sometime early in the divorce process and ends at the time the divorce becomes final.

As mentioned in Chapter 3, when you're using ADR one of your first tasks is to create a Temporary Agreement to cover immediate issues. Temporary Spousal Support is one of those issues. To determine the need for Spousal Support, estimate what each spouse's monthly income and expenses will be during the time the divorce is pending. Try to come up with a payment amount that will help meet the receiving spouse's needs during this time while being fair to the paying spouse.

Keep in mind that the amount you agree on for temporary support payments may not be perfect. It is just the best solution you can both come up with at the time. If the amount turns out to be too high or too low, you can discuss it again and agree to adjust it. Another possibility is to correct for the overpayment or underpayment when you divide your assets and debts.

Post-Divorce Spousal Support

After the divorce is final, monthly spousal support payments may still be needed. The typical reason is to bridge the gap between a spouse's present and future ability to earn an income.

Here's a typical example. During their marriage, Jim had a high-paying career, while Diane focused on caring for the home and family. After the divorce, Diane needs to find a job so she can support herself, but that is no easy task. She has been out of the workforce for 15 years and lacks experience, references, and up-to-date skills. To avoid being limited to low-paying jobs, she needs to prepare for a career. She may need to take classes or even go back to school full time, and she needs time to search for employment. Post-Divorce Spousal Support allows her these opportunities.

Post-Divorce Spousal Support is seldom permanent. Once the receiving spouse is earning sufficient income, the support payments are typically no longer needed.

Factors Affecting Spousal Support

When using ADR, you and your spouse work together to come to an agreement about Spousal Support. However, it is helpful to know how a judge might decide the issue if your case went to court. Having this information will help you set realistic expectations as you enter into negotiations.

That said, there is no standard process for deciding Spousal Support. Not only do states have different laws, but no state has a set formula, since every couple's situation is unique. However, certain factors are considered in most states. They include:

Legal limits. State laws may limit the amount or duration of Spousal Support. For example, in some states the monthly payments cannot exceed a certain dollar amount or a certain percentage of the paying spouse's income. Some states require that Spousal Support ends when the receiving spouse remarries or cohabitates with another person.

Income. Spousal Support is necessary if one spouse is a high-wage earner and the other is not. If both spouses make about the same amount of money, spousal support would not necessarily be needed.

Other resources. If the spouse requesting support has other income streams, such as dividends or Social Security benefits, that income is generally factored into any spousal support calculation. In some cases, this factor could decrease or even eliminate the need for Spousal Support.

Contributions to the marriage. In the example given previously, the stay-at-home wife contributed greatly to the education, training, and increased earning capacity of the husband. This would be a significant factor in the award of Spousal Support.

Age and health. Suppose the husband has a permanent disability or a serious, long-lasting illness that limits his ability to get a job. Not only would he receive Spousal Support, but if the state has time limits for receiving those payments, the judge would probably lift them. The same would be true if the receiving spouse is too old to reenter the workforce.

Duration of the marriage. Typically, the shorter the marriage, the shorter the duration of spousal support payments and the smaller the amount.

Education or training needs. How long has the receiving spouse been out of the workforce? What skills does he or she have? To get back into the workforce, is it necessary to get a college degree, or only take a couple of refresher courses? This can affect the amount and duration of Spousal Support.

Child custody arrangements. After the divorce, one of the parents may be primarily responsible for the care of a young or disabled child. That parent will need to balance this responsibility with the need to make a living. For example, the parent would need a job that is located close to the child and does not require frequent travel. A flexible work schedule would be needed so that the parent could take the child to doctor appointments, pick the child up from school, and so on. These requirements would impact the ability to find a job and the amount of earnings. Child support payments do not take these factors into account, so additional spousal support may be needed.

Assets, debts, and other obligations. Let's say that during the marriage, the wife was the high-wage earner and the husband stayed at home with the kids. In settling their divorce, they agree that the husband will be the primary parent and the wife will make child support payments to him. In addition, she will assume most of the responsibility for paying off the large amount of debt they had accumulated. If she also has to make large spousal support payments, she might not have enough money left to meet her own reasonable financial needs. A judge would take that into account when deciding on Spousal Support.

Standard of living during the marriage. Some states put a lot of emphasis on this factor. The premise is that if the spouses became accustomed to a certain high-end lifestyle during the marriage, it is unfair for the high-earning spouse to continue that lifestyle while the other cannot. Most states, however, focus on meeting reasonable or basic needs of the receiving spouse rather than maintaining a high standard of living.

Marital misconduct. Spousal Support is not designed to compensate for a bad marriage. But what if one of the spouses spent considerable marital assets to buy illegal drugs or have an affair? A judge would probably award additional Spousal Support to the non-offending spouse to make up for the marital assets that were wasted. Spousal Support could also be affected if one of the spouses had committed family violence.

Other factors. When awarding Spousal Support, a judge can consider any other factors relating to the economic circumstances of the spouses. In essence, this means the final decision is left to the judge's discretion.

That last item is the wild card. If you take your divorce to court, you really do not know what the judge is going to do. That is why you want to continue to pursue ADR methods instead of going to court. While you might think every factor listed above falls to your favor, you could be wrong. The judge may order you to pay more spousal support and for a longer period of time than you want, or you may not receive the spousal support you expect. So take an honest look at these factors and your own circumstances, use the proven methods of ADR that are available to you, and reach an agreement. Do not give up control of your future or finances to a judge.

Negotiating Spousal Support

In order to negotiate Spousal Support, you will need to know the laws in your state. Seek out the advice of an attorney to see what factors are relevant in your state and what legal limitations or requirements you will have to follow.

You and your spouse will also need to share your financial information, such as paycheck stubs, money market account statements, trust documents, and so on.

If you are requesting Spousal Support, try to figure out what your monthly income and expenses will be after the divorce. This will help you see how much additional income you will need to fill the gap. If you don't have a job or want to find a better paying one, this would be a good time to draft a résumé and check with an employment agency or recruiter to see what jobs are available for your current skill set. If retraining or further education is required, try to find information about where you could get it, how long it would take, and how much it would cost.

If you are expecting to pay Spousal Support, estimating your future budget and resources is just as important for you. Your spouse's need for support must be balanced against your ability to make the payments.

Once all this information has been gathered and shared, you have what you need to start negotiating. Bring your requests to the table, but be open to compromise based on the factors described earlier. To keep your negotiations peaceful, remember the ground rules from Chapter 6. If you are using Mediation, the mediator can walk you through the negotiations on Spousal Support. If you're using Collaborative Law, your attorney and perhaps other professionals are available to help you get through this issue.

Mediator's Perspective
Think. Solve. Settle.

When people are going through a divorce, one of the first questions I ask is: What are you afraid of? Many times they are afraid of being alone. For those with kids they are afraid of the effect of the divorce on the children. And for the spouse who is financially dependent on the other spouse, it's the fear of not being able to pay the bills.

I mediated a case where a couple had been married for 21 years. Before having children, the wife was employed as an x-ray technician. When the couple was expecting their first child they decided the wife would become a stay-at-home mom. This arrangement allowed the husband to build a very good, lucrative career. While the husband made good money and had put money into retirement funds they had no other savings. The lack of savings hindered wife's ability to be financially stable after the divorce.

Everyone was aware that the wife would need a job and develop a career after the divorce. She wanted to go back into the medical field, but the 21 year gap in employment would require her to completely retrain and obtain additional education. The wife had done her homework before Mediation so was able to show it would take about three years to get the necessary education to reenter the medical field.

During the mediation I worked with the wife on her budget. We calculated the cost of tuition for retraining, the cost of the living expenses during the retraining and the time it would take for her to acquire the necessary certifications for the field she wanted. The ultimate goal was to provide the wife financial security while she built sufficient job security.

We determined during her first year of training, she would not be able to work and complete her educational requirements. So, we calculated her monthly expenses, cost of tuition and books and certification exams without any income. We all worked together during mediation and the husband and the wife reached an agreement. She would receive spousal support in the amount of $3,500 a month

Next, the wife determined she could work part-time during her second year of training. This would bring in some income while she built her skills and continued with her education. This part-time job would pay $10 an hour for about 25 hours per week. This generated approximately a monthly income of $825. Based on this, the husband and the wife agreed to spousal support in the amount of $2,750 per month for the second year.

For the third year, the wife assumed she could get a full-time job in her field. However, even with the full-time job she would be unable to completely pay for all of her bills. The husband and the wife agreed to supplement her full-time income at a rate of $1,000 per month for the third year.

The most important thing the wife brought to mediation was information. From that information we were able to help establish a reasonable basic financial forecast for her during her retraining. With this information, we were all able to negotiate a solution to Spousal Support in logical steps and a reasoned approach.

Finalizing the Spousal Support Agreement

Like all divorce agreements, the spousal support agreement will need to be in writing. Most likely it will be included in the overall agreement you reach on all issues. Make sure that everything you have agreed to makes it into the Final Agreement. Otherwise, it does not exist.

Summing Up

Spousal Support is not intended to be a financial windfall for one spouse or a financial penalty for the other. It is intended to help a spouse avoid, if possible, the devastating financial impact of divorce. Each couple will have unique factors and circumstances that will need to be analyzed in determining spousal support. Be open to discussion. Realize that discussing money is always stressful, even more now in the context of a divorce. Whichever ADR process you are using, approach this topic openly and with the intent to be fair.

Getting a divorce is scary, especially for those spouses who are dependent on the other spouse for their financial security. This fear can pervade a great deal of the negotiations on spousal support. Be willing to listen, to understand, and to overcome these obstacles with respect.

12

Child Custody

If you bungle raising your children, I don't think
whatever else you do well matters very much.

Jacqueline Kennedy Onassis

While every issue arising from a divorce is difficult to work
through, child custody is often the most contentious. It has
the most devastating effect on the kids, since they usually find
themselves caught in the middle.

That's why it's so important to approach this issue ratio-
nally. Don't put yourself, your spouse, and especially your
kids through the heartache of a custody battle. Instead, use
ADR to find solutions that are in your children's best interest.

Defining Custody Terms

Many couples fight over child custody arrangements
without knowing exactly what they are fighting for. Often
they do not understand the terminology that is used in child
custody cases. For example, many divorcing parents come

to court asking for "full custody," but are unable to explain exactly what that means. So before you discuss custody with your spouse, make sure you both understand what the terms mean and how different custody arrangements work.

Basically, there are two ways to categorize custody. The first has to do with the types of rights and responsibilities that are involved: legal or physical.

- *Legal custody* identifies who is responsible for making important decisions about the child's welfare.
- *Physical custody* defines where the child will live on a regular basis.

For each type of custody, legal and physical, two options are available: joint or sole.

- *Joint* means custody is shared by both parents.
- *Sole* means custody is held by one parent. However, as we'll discuss later, in most cases the other parent is not completely out of the picture.

To accurately describe a custody situation, you need to specify both dimensions: whether you're talking about legal or physical custody, and whether it's joint or sole. That's why the phrase "sole custody" by itself doesn't make sense. So for example, parents might agree that one of them will be given Sole Physical Custody, but they will share Joint Legal Custody. We'll explain more about what these terms mean as we go along; but for now, at least you know more about custody than many divorcing couples do.

Just to make things more complicated, the terminology may differ depending on the laws of your state. For example, instead of legal custody and physical custody, Texas uses the terms "conservatorship" and "possession and access." In this book, we'll stick with the term "custody" for the sake of consistency. An attorney can help you understand the specific laws in your state.

Custody Evaluations

If you are using an ADR method a Custody Evaluation is usually not needed. However, there are times during ADR that a Custody Evaluation would be a valuable resource from which negotiations can begin.

A custody evaluator is a qualified individual, usually a licensed professional counselor, who will examine the dynamics of the family and whose ultimate responsibility is to prepare a report making recommendations on child custody, visitation and any other issue that has arisen during the divorce.

To prepare the report and recommendations, the evaluator will interview both spouses, the children, and others who live in homes where the children live or visit. They may also interview doctors of the children or parents, teachers or school personnel and other references. In addition, the evaluator may have each parent and/or the children take a psychological evaluation depending on the specific issues in the case.

Remember if the case goes to court these reports are provided to the judge to review, meaning they may be public record viewable at the courthouse by anyone, unless specifically sealed by the court. Most importantly, while the evaluator makes recommendation to the court it is completely within the court's discretion to adopt the recommendations, adopt some of the recommendations or ignore the recommendations completely. A full Custody Evaluation can cost upwards of $20,000 and it is merely a recommendation to the parties or judge or arbitrator.

Even though the evaluator is only providing recommendations, a Custody Evaluation can be of significant assistance to parents attempting to settle their case outside of court. The evaluation provides for an independent third person to listen to each parent's concerns, have those concerns investigated and to have recommendations prepared based on the results of the examination.

The report also provides the attorneys in the case an indication of how the custody trial may play out in court if they were not able to settle outside of court to determine if their client's expectations are reasonable.

With all the benefits a Custody Evaluation may have, it is still a very expensive tool. In the end, you will have to decide whether the benefit of having this information is worth the cost.

Legal Custody

Legal Custody gives one or both parents responsibility for making decisions important to a child's life. Examples of these decisions include whether the child will attend public or private school, what medications the child will take, whether the child should see a counselor or psychiatrist, and what type of religious upbringing the child will have.

Courts and legislatures in most states prefer Joint Legal Custody so that parents will share in making these important decisions. Joint Legal Custody makes sense. While the parents are married, they both have to make decisions about the child. After they are divorced, the same decisions have to be made. No matter how mad Dad is at Mom, or vice versa, both parents should have a say in decisions about their child. Having both parents involved as much as possible in the child's life is, more often than not, in the child's best interest.

It's also beneficial for the parents, who both have the satisfaction of knowing their opinion must be considered before major decisions about the child are made.

If you and your spouse agree on Joint Legal Custody, discuss how you will make decisions about your child. Options include giving each parent the right to make decisions independently; allowing each parent to make a decision after receiving input (but not necessarily agreement) from the other parent; or requiring that both parents must agree. You may want to specify different options for different types of decisions. For example, you might agree to make medical decisions together but designate one parent to make educational decisions. Also negotiate how you will notify each other when the need for a decision arises, which forms of communication are acceptable (email, text, cell phone), and what to do in case of emergency.

Joint Legal Custody may not work for everyone. It depends on how well you and your spouse can get along and communicate. If every decision causes an argument, or if decisions are delayed for days or weeks because you cannot agree, the child will suffer. In that case, Sole Legal Custody may be a better option.

Usually, however, Sole Legal Custody is reserved for cases where a parent is deemed unfit. Factors to consider include a history of family violence, mental instability, drug or alcohol addiction, neglect of the child, or abandonment. If these factors can be proven, then it is appropriate for the other parent to have the exclusive right to make decisions about the child's welfare and well-being.

Physical Custody

Simply put, Physical Custody refers to where the child will live on a regular basis. The person or persons with Physical Custody of a child have the legal right to have the child live with them.

While our goal is to keep you out of court, it is helpful to know what factors a judge would consider when deciding on Physical Custody. You and your spouse could analyze the same factors as you prepare to negotiate. While this list is not exhaustive, the factors include:

- Which parent has been the primary caretaker of the child during the marriage.
- The physical and emotional health of the parents.
- The past and present relationship the child has with each parent.
- Whether both parents have a history of spending a lot of time with the child.
- Which home is the child used to.
- Adjustment to school and other activities.
- The support network that is available to each parent and the child.
- Cultural and religious differences.
- Disciplinary techniques used by both parents.
- Financial ability for the parent to support the household.
- In some instances, the child's wishes.

That last factor, the child's wishes, is a very touchy subject. We are by no means advising that you ask your child which parent they would rather live with or, worse yet, which parent they love more. That would be a horrible thing to ask. Instead, we suggest that you and your spouse discuss the child's wishes without involving the child. For example, you can talk with each other about whether your daughter is happy in her current school and has close friends in her neighborhood. That's far better than asking your daughter where she wants to live. Be smart. Be careful. If you need professional advice about the best way to evaluate the child's wishes, find a counselor who can guide you. Once you put the child in the middle of the decision making, the damage has been done.

Joint Physical Custody

When parents have Joint Physical Custody, the child lives with each parent for a substantial amount of time. This does not necessarily mean that the child's time with each parent will be exactly equal, but it is as balanced as possible. The parents agree on a schedule for when each of them will have the child. Both of them are involved in the child's day-to-day life, and they share responsibility for the child's physical care.

For Joint Physical Custody to work, the parents must communicate well. They should also live relatively close to one another.

The overriding benefit of Joint Physical Custody is that both parents are involved as much as possible in the child's life. More often than not, this is in the child's best interest. The most important relationships in a child's life are with Mom and Dad, and this custody arrangement maximizes the amount of time spent with each of them.

Joint Physical Custody can also benefit the parents. Neither of them is alone in raising the child. There will be times when one parent is better equipped to advise the child on a certain matter, whether it's how to understand a math problem, how to handle a bully, or how to drive a car. When one parent is traveling for work or just needs a break, arrangements can be made for the other parent to take care of the child.

However, Joint Physical Custody also has disadvantages. In essence, the child has two homes rather than one. Constantly going back and forth between them may be stressful. Where will I be next weekend? Where do I keep my stuff? Who is going to help me with homework? Where do I fit in to Mom's new family or Dad's new family? In addition, having two homes might cause confusion over the child's address when it comes to enrolling in school, getting mail, getting a driver's license, and registering to vote. These are not insurmountable problems, but they can make life more complicated than it already is.

Sole Physical Custody

Sole Physical Custody means the child primarily lives with one parent and visits with the other parent. For example, a couple might agree that the child will reside with Mom during the week and stay with Dad on the weekend. In that case, Mom would be designated as having Sole Physical Custody. In most states, she would be referred to as the custodial parent and Dad would be the noncustodial parent.

As you can see from the example, the term "sole" is a bit misleading. Sole Physical Custody does not mean that the noncustodial parent will not have any contact with the child. On the contrary, visits occur at regular intervals that are laid out in a visitation schedule. The parents can decide when visits will occur and for how long. Even if the noncustodial parent has a serious problem such as drug abuse, visits will still take place, although they will probably be limited and supervised. Chapter 13 explains how to come up with a schedule and provides several examples.

Unfortunately, people often react negatively to the idea of Sole Physical Custody. They associate it with the image of an unfit parent: "He must think I'm a bad mother," or "She doesn't trust me to take care of our son." This is simply not the case. There are good reasons to give one parent Sole Physical Custody, and they have nothing to do with parenting abilities.

Sole Physical Custody offers a way around the drawbacks of Joint Physical Custody. Practically speaking, it is easier for the child to have one residence than two. Spending more time in one home is calmer than constantly switching from one house to the other. There is no confusion about the child's address or school district, and it can be easier to manage the child's school schedule and extra activities.

If one parent has Sole Physical Custody of the child, this designation is not intended to be a slight on the other parent. It does not mean one parent is better than the other; it's just a matter of geography.

Many parents spend an enormous amount of effort, time, and money to "win" Sole Physical Custody or to avoid being the noncustodial parent. Do not fall into that trap. Your relationship with your child will not be based on labels. It will be based on mutual respect, love, and understanding.

Relocation/Geographical Restriction

When a parent has Sole Physical Custody, another consideration that affects physical custody is if a parent has the right to move with the child and establish his residence.

With very few exceptions the child's interest is best served when the child has reasonable access to both parents. Reasonable access is more difficult the further away the parents live from each other. That is why states allow for relocation restrictions. A Relocation Restrictions prevents the custodial parent from establishing a residence for the child outside a specified geographical area. This restriction remains in place unless the other parent (noncustodial parent) of the child moves outside that same geographical area.

For example, Mom, who is the custodial parent, and child live in Cooke County, Illinois. There is a Relocation Restriction preventing Mom from moving the child outside Cooke County, Illinois and contiguous counties.

Since the purpose is to keep the child close to both parents, relocation restrictions also impacts the noncustodial parent (the parent who exercises visitation). If the noncustodial parent moves from the geographically defined area the restriction is lifted.

In this example, if Mom is geographically restricted to Cook County and contiguous counties and Dad takes a job and moves to Wyoming the Relocation Restriction is lifted, which allows mom and child to move anywhere they want. It makes sense. The purpose of the restriction is to keep the child geographically close to both parents. If the other parent leaves the area, the purpose is out the window.

Relocation restrictions are great to keep parents and child together. However, they do cause problems. If Dad finds a job of a lifetime out-of-state and he wants to take it, the Relocation Restriction will be lifted. If Mom remarries and the new husband lives out of state, if she has a Relocation Restriction in place then she can move, but the child can't.

This is another issue that will need to be discussed with your mediator, attorney or arbitrator. Leaving the matter to the courts is not worth much. Individual judges have individual opinions as to whether or not to impose a Relocation Restriction or not. Think about it and how it fits or does not fit your specific situation. If you cannot agree you can settle all the other issues and leave this one issue to the arbitrator or judge. Your child is best served, however, by having his parents decide.

Injunctions

In order to preserve the peace, to protect one or both parents, or to protect the kids, it is sometimes necessary to agree to or impose injunctions. An Injunction is a court order requiring a person to either not do certain acts or to do certain acts. Some examples of injunctions would be: (1) to prohibit the parents from drinking alcohol while in possession of the children; (2) to prohibit either parent from having a person with whom they are romantically involved from spending the night when the parent is in possession of the children; (3) to prohibit a parent from introducing the children to romantic partners for a period of six months; and, (4) to prohibit the parents from making disparaging remarks about the other parent to the children. These are only a few of the possible injunctions that can be used to alleviate fears of the parents about the other parent's conduct and to provide a set of basic rules for conduct around the children.

Injunction can be very effective in addressing specific, perceived problems during and after a divorce. Parents can agree on injunctions during ADR, but in order to enforce injunctions a parent would have to go to court.

Rights of Parents

Whatever custody arrangement you agree on, every parent has certain rights when it comes to their kids; unless otherwise restricted by a court order. These rights include the right to:

- Receive information from the other parent concerning the child's health, education, and welfare.
- Access the child's medical, dental, psychological, and educational records.
- Consult with a physician, dentist, or psychologist who is treating the child.
- Consult with school officials about the child's welfare, educational status, and school activities.
- Attend school activities.
- Be designated on the child's records as a person to be notified in case of an emergency.
- Consent to medical, dental, and surgical treatment during an emergency involving an immediate danger to the health and safety of the child.
- Manage the estate of the child, to the extent the estate has been created by the parent or the parent's family.

In addition, when the child is in the possession of a parent, that parent has specific rights and duties. These include:
- The duty to care for, control, protect, and reasonably discipline the child.
- The duty to support the child with clothing, food, shelter, and medical and dental care.
- The right to consent to medical and dental care.
- The right to direct the moral and religious training of the child.

Unless a court finds the parent is unfit or cannot reasonably act in the child's best interest, the rights and duties are presumed. Still, they should be specified in your child custody agreement. Appendix Q provides a Parental Rights Duty Worksheet.

Judge's Perspective
If They Could Only Dream Big

In my job as a judge, it becomes necessary to bring kids whose parents are going through a divorce into my office and talk with them. I learn a lot from these kids. Often they are smarter than their parents. They plainly see the dysfunction in their house. They see the problems their parents are facing. They identify with specificity how things could get better. They have grown up faster than they should have.

By accident I began to ask kids, without any limitations whatsoever: "If I gave you a magic wand and you could wish for anything you wanted, what would it be?"

If you were to ask my oldest son this open-ended question, he would say that he wants to be the first five-star general in the United States Marine Corps. Ask my middle son, and he would say he wants to own a video game store. Ask my youngest son, and he would say he wants to play in the National Football League. When I was a kid, I dreamed of going to space, playing professional soccer, and becoming President of the United States.

The kids in my office, almost without exception say, "I just want Mom and Dad to get along." That's it. Nothing more, nothing less. It is really sad.

What I have determined is that kids who are in the midst of a contentious divorce or custody fight cannot dream big. They cannot dream big because their minimum basic emotional needs are not being met. They are insecure about what is going on in their family. They are afraid of

(Continued)

their uncertain futures. They are caught in the middle of their fighting parents, often being asked the most preposterous things: Do you want to live with your mom or me? What is your dad doing when I am not around? What does your mom say about me? Why don't you want to live with me? And then there is all the fighting when Mom and Dad are together.

These kids want what we all want: a sense of security and peace.

You don't need money to give your kids the only thing they want—for Mom and Dad to get along. It may cost you a little pride. You may have to bite your tongue. But don't you think it's worth it?

Do everything you possibly can to get along with the other parent. Your kids deserve it. Let them know that everything is okay and that they can dream as big as ever!

For younger kids, I would recommend *Meet Max Books* authored by Jennifer Leister. These books help explain divorce in a kid appropriate way. You can find them at www. meetmaxbooks.com.

Summing Up

Often times, couples fight over custody with no solid grounds or argument to do so. Some warring parents believe the designation as joint this or sole that is some indication as to who the better parent is or who the worse parent is. As a result, they will fight to the death—or to financial ruin—to "win" one designation or another.

In these types of fights, there are no winners. However, there is a loser—your child. Before running off and spending thousands of dollars and many tears over what each parent will be legally designated, be sure you understand the terms you are throwing around. Knowing what you know now should give you enough information to get started.

Use ADR to reach the best agreement you can for yourselves and your child. As always, follow the ground rules explained in Chapter 6. Keep an open mind and think outside of the box. Remember that a child custody determination must focus on what is in the best interest of the child, not the parents.

At the same time, remember that as long as the child is safe, all parents have a right to be involved in their child's life. No matter what happens in the divorce, Mom will always be Mom and Dad will always be Dad. The influence from both parents is important.

Don't get bogged down in legal jargon. "Sole" and "joint" are just words. What matters is your actions. Focus on what you both can do to be the best parents you can be.

13

Visitation Schedules

Your children need your presence more than your presents.

Jesse Jackson

In the busy world in which we live, it is difficult enough to spend the time we want to with our children. In a divorced family, it is even harder.

When you were married, you were able to see your kids every day, ask them how they were doing, have dinner with them, help them with their homework, and tuck them into bed. As a divorced parent, you will probably not be able to participate in these activities every single day. This does not mean you're a bad parent; it is just the normal process of divorce.

Still, divorced parents want to spend as much time with their kids as possible. That's completely understandable, and it's another issue to be worked out with ADR.

Visitation and ADR

The previous chapter discussed custody, including the right to have physical custody of your children. Visitation schedules go hand-in-hand with that issue. The term "visitation" (also known as parenting time or possession) refers to the period of time when each parent has access to their children. In other words, you and your spouse will need to map out a schedule for when the children will spend time with each of you.

If you can't agree on a visitation schedule, the decision will be made by an arbitrator or a judge. Some states have laws that define standard schedules the judge can put in place. These may work fine in some cases, but more often than not the visitation plan needs to be individually tailored to the specific situation of the family. The schedule must accommodate the parents' jobs, the children's school schedule, their extracurricular activities, and other time demands. On top of that, the schedule should address the desire for both parents to spend time with their kids—and vice versa, as well as the children's need for consistency and some semblance of normalcy. It is a difficult challenge.

Trying to get a highly customized visitation schedule from a judge in court is almost impossible. The judge's limited time and the inability to know or learn the specific ins-and-outs of a family's schedule makes this too tall of a task. Although the judge tries as best as he or she can, it probably will not work out to the parents' or children's favor.

The better approach is to use ADR to work out the schedule. If you're using the IHOP method, you and your spouse can try to work it out together. In this chapter we will give you guidance on what factors to consider, examples of different types of schedules you can use, and other tools for developing a mutually agreeable schedule. If you are using Mediation, Collaborative Law, or Arbitration, you will have access to lawyers and mediators who have extensive experience in family law cases and have dealt with these issues. They can take the time to help you create a customized schedule for your situation.

Your Kids Need Both Parents

Some of you might be thinking that your spouses are completely incapable of caring for children. They can barely take care of themselves! Perhaps that's true. Unfortunately, that ship has sailed. The most important parenting decision you can make is choosing the person you want to have a child with. Once that decision is made, nothing you or anyone else can do will change who the other parent of your child is. Whoever it is, your child has a right to know and bond with both parents.

Maybe you think your spouse doesn't know the right way to raise children. Just remember: no one is born knowing how to be a good parent. We all learn by doing.

It's essential that you do everything in your control to make sure your children have a chance to know, bond with, and love the other parent. Your spouse should do the same. Both parents need to take part in every aspect of raising their children. You may think it's not in your best interest to have the other parent around the children, but that's not the standard we are governed by. The entire focus in a divorce case involving children is to determine what is in their best interest, not the parents.

Define Your Needs

The first step in this journey is to discuss the individual needs and goals that your visitation schedule must meet. Of course each parent wants to spend as much time as possible with the children. But to make a workable schedule, you need to consider the factors that affect your particular situation.

Start by looking at your own schedules. What are your work hours? Do you travel as part of your work? What other activities might affect the amount of time you can spend with your children? Make sure your answers are realistic. The worst thing you could do is agree to a visitation plan that you can't keep because it doesn't fit in with your schedule.

Also gather and share information about the children's daily schedules. Consider their school hours, extracurricular activities, regular doctor's appointments, driver's education classes, and so on. You'll want to create a visitation plan that does not disrupt these activities.

Evaluate other factors that may affect your visitation schedule. For example, how far do you live from the other parent? How well do you communicate with each other? Once you have identified your needs as best as you can, you are ready to start considering your options for visitation.

Examples of Visitation Schedules

The following are examples of common visitation schedules and the arguments for and against each one. If you are using IHOP, try discussing these as a starting point. If you are going to Mediation, your mediator will know about these possibilities and many more. If you are going to an arbitrator or the court, one of these schedules may be imposed on your family.

Standard Schedule

As mentioned earlier, some states have standard visitation schedules that are set out by the state's legislature. They are intended to be a legislative mandate of what visitation schedule is in the best interest of most children. If you live in one of those states, the statutory visitation schedule is a good starting point for most negotiations. Such schedules work well for a lot of families, but don't get hung up on the standard schedule if it does not work for your family's specific situation. Legislators have no way of knowing what each individual family needs.

Obviously, you'll need to find out the details of your state's standard schedule (if there is one). Most standard schedules assume that the children spend the majority of their time with one parent (the custodial parent). The other (noncustodial) parent exercises visitation.

Here's a typical example. In the schedule shown below, the noncustodial parent has the children:

- Every Wednesday evening, from 6 p.m. to 8 p.m.
- Every other weekend, beginning at 6 p.m. Friday and ending at 6 p.m. Sunday.

Sun	Mon	Tue	Wed	Thu	Fri	Sat
A	A	A	A/B*/A	A	A/B	B
B/A	A	A	A/B*/A	A	A	A
A	A	A	A/B*/A	A	A/B	B
B/A	A	A	A/B*/A	A	A	A

A = custodial parent
B = noncustodial parent
*6 p.m. to 8 p.m.

- Alternating holidays. For example, one year the non-custodial parent would have the children during the first part of Thanksgiving weekend and the last part of the school's Christmas vacation. The next year, the holiday schedule would be reversed.
- Four weeks during the summer (or a similar period, such as 30 days).

This type of schedule has several benefits. It provides children stability during the week, which is important for school. They will still move from house to house, but this is a product of the divorce, not the visitation schedule. The standard schedule usually works well for working parents.

However, the schedule does have some drawbacks. It doesn't give the children substantial time with the noncustodial parent. It also requires the parents to have frequent contact in order to exchange the children, which may be a problem if they don't get along well. If the parents live some distance from each other, the children will spend a lot of time going back and forth in the car and therefore, will have less quality time with the noncustodial parent.

Expanded Weekend Possession

Some states have an expanded weekend possession schedule that the noncustodial parent can choose. It might work like this:

- The parents alternate weekends. On the noncustodial parent's weekend, the period of visitation starts at the time school dismisses on Thursday and ends at the time school starts on Monday.
- During the rest of that week, the custodial parent has the children until school dismisses on Thursday. The

noncustodial parent then has visitation until school starts Friday morning.

- Holidays are handled the same way as the standard schedule.
- Summer visitation lasts longer than in the standard schedule. For example, it might be extended to five weeks or 40 days.

This type of schedule addresses several of the downsides of the standard visitation schedule. It gives the noncustodial parent more visitation time, so that the balance of time for each parent is closer to equal. It also decreases contact between the parents, since the exchanges occur at school. Like the standard schedule, this schedule won't work as well if the parents don't live close to each other. See Appendix P for more Expanded Weekends Sample Language.

Sun	Mon	Tue	Wed	Thu	Fri	Sat
A	A	A	A	A/B	B	B
B	B/A	A	A	A/B	B/A	A
A	A	A	A	A/B	B	B
B	B/A	A	A	A/B	B/A	A

A = custodial parent
B = noncustodial parent

Extra Holidays and Summer Time

Between the parents' work schedules and the kids' school schedules, it is often difficult to carve out additional time for anything else, including visitation. Holidays and summer breaks offer the opportunity for additional parenting time that usually does not interfere with work and school. Therefore, you may want to consider letting children spend extra holidays and additional summer time with the noncustodial parent.

We know what you may be thinking: the noncustodial parent has the fun time, and the custodial parent has the time that requires the most work. You are certainly right, but this visitation plan is a trade-off, just like everything else. It's merely one option of many. Be creative in negotiating, and think outside of the box about ways to achieve both parents' goals.

Alternating Weeks

If you and your spouse get along fairly well, live close together, and want your time with your kids to be as equal as possible, you may want to explore the concept of an alternating weeks schedule (sometimes called week on/week off). The schedule is simple: each parent has the children for a full week. The exchange always takes place at the same time, such as 6 p.m. every Sunday. If you label the parents A and B, the schedule looks like this:

Sun	Mon	Tue	Wed	Thu	Fri	Sat
B/A	A	A	A	A	A	A
A/B	B	B	B	B	B	B
B/A	A	A	A	A	A	A

Using this schedule, the children have equal time with both parents. Staying in one place for a full week provides stability, with fewer trips back and forth. On the other hand, the week-long stay can also be a disadvantage, since the children go seven days without seeing one of the parents.

If the kids are young and not yet in school, the alternating weeks schedule can work well. Spending a full week with each parent allows the children to develop close bonds with both of them, an important part of early childhood development. The schedule is relatively easy to handle at this age because there is no need to contend with school schedules.

Once kids start school, the alternating weeks plan becomes more difficult to manage. Both parents are responsible for getting the children to and from school and extracurricular activities during their respective week. If one parent lives far from the children's school, getting there on time can be difficult.

Both parents must also coordinate long-term school projects. For example, suppose the science fair is coming up. Creating a good science project takes planning and a lot of work over time. It can't be done in a day. If the children spend one week with one parent and the next week with the other, all of them will need to stay in communication about what has been done and what still needs to be done.

During holidays parents usually will alternate the major holidays each year. For example, one parent will have the first part of Thanksgiving and Thanksgiving Day and the time after Christmas in even years and the second half of Thanksgiving and the first part of Christmas and Christmas Day the next year. Other religions will have different holidays that will need to be addressed when discussion about visitation comes up. The more customized you need the visitation schedule to be, for whatever reason, the more your case should be settled using ADR.

A lot of times parents using alternating weeks will carry this schedule throughout the entire year, including summers. However, some parents schedule extended summer breaks with their children. For example, the first year one parent would get the choice of taking a week that would not normally be theirs. Once that parent makes his or her choice, the other parent can designate a week that would not normally be theirs. That would result in each parent having the children for three weeks during the summer. There are many ways to work through summer visitation depending on the time available to the parents and the children.

In short, managing the alternating weeks schedule can be a challenge with school-age children, but under the right circumstances, with good communication, it is certainly not impossible. See Appendix O for Alternative Weeks (Week On / Week Off) Sample Language.

2/2/3

The 2/2/3 visitation schedule also gives each parent 50% of the time, but using a different approach. One parent has possession of the children on Mondays and Tuesdays. The other parent has the children on Wednesdays and Thursdays. Fridays, Saturdays, and Sundays alternate between the parents. Here's how it looks:

Sun	Mon	Tue	Wed	Thu	Fri	Sat
B	B/A	A	A/B	B	B/A	A
A	A	A	A/B	B	B	B
B	B/A	A	A/B	B	B/A	A

In the chart above it is assumed the parents will pick-up and drop-off the children at school. One parent dropping off the children in the morning at the end of their period of possession and the other parent picking the children up from school at the beginning of theirs. If the children are not in school, other arrangements would need to be made regarding the location of the pick-up and drop-off location.

Compared to the Alternating Weeks Schedule, the 2/2/3 schedule lets the children see each parent more often. It does require more pick-ups and drop-offs, but can be workable under the right circumstances and with the right kids. Children in this type of schedule must be able to cope with the constant movement and change.

Like the Alternating Weeks Schedule, a 2/2/3 schedule does not work well unless the parents and children can communicate effectively. They will need to coordinate their activities so that homework gets done, PE clothes get washed, the kids get to sports practice, and so on. It takes a very committed family to make a 2/2/3 schedule work effectively. See Appendix N for 2/2/3 Possession Schedule Sample Language.

Visitation Schedules for Infants and Toddlers

The first few weeks and months of an infant's life are incredibly important. During this time, infants create bonds with their parents and other caregivers. A parent who is in contact with the baby only every other week or every other weekend does not have enough opportunity to hold, feed, and play with the baby—the very activities that allow the infant to identify and become attached to the parent.

In addition, infants do not have the concept of time that older children have. They need frequent, short periods of visitation in order to have positive contact with both parents on a regular basis. It can be difficult to schedule frequent visitation that accommodates parents' work schedules while also maintaining a predictable feeding and sleep schedule for the infant. But, it's extremely important to focus on the baby's best interests in these first few months.

As babies grow and eventually becomes toddlers, their needs change. Therefore, the visitation schedule must change as well. Here are some schedules that we have found appropriate for specific ages:

Birth to six months. The noncustodial parent should have two to three separate visitation periods per week, each lasting three to six hours.

Six to twelve months. Add longer periods of visitation (up to eight hours) on Saturday or Sunday.

Twelve to eighteen months. As the child starts to become more independent, additional visitation time is appropriate and important. The schedule might consist of six-hour periods of visitation two to three times per week. In addition, overnight visitation periods can be introduced, such as every other weekend from Noon Saturday to Noon Sunday.

Eighteen months to three years. Continue to increase visitation time every six months until the child is ready for a more "traditional" visitation schedule, usually around the age of three.

Whatever you and your spouse craft for your infant, the goal should be to establish a strong, caring relationship between the child and both parents.

Children with Special Needs

Some kids aren't quite ready for a standard schedule, and those with conditions such as Asperger's syndrome may need a different schedule to thrive. In these instances, it might be helpful to bring in a specialist in education or special needs to help design a more tailored visitation schedule for the individual child.

Mediation and Collaborative Law Provide an effective mechanism for such discussions to play out. The mediator can sit down with the specialist and the parents to come up with the best possible schedule. In the Collaborative Law setting, the specialist is included as part of the team and works with everyone to come up with the best solution.

On the other hand, if your divorce went to court, you and your spouse might each have to retain and pay for your own specialist. Those specialists would be called to the stand as expert witnesses. After listening to their testimony, the judge would decide whether to adopt the recommendations of one expert, combine the opinions of both experts, or order something completely different. This is another great example of why visitation disputes do not belong in court.

Will You Stick to the Schedule?

Whatever visitation schedule you are considering, make sure you can carry it out. Many parents come to court and ask for, and often fight for, the most visitation possible, but their own work schedule interferes with their ability to exercise all the visitation they are asking for.

Not exercising the ordered or agreed to visitation can come back to haunt you. Assume Dad had been given a schedule that he can't carry out. Years later he gets into a dispute with Mom about a medical decision concerning the child, and they take it to court. The cross-examination of Dad would go something like this:

> **Attorney**: Dad, you are here today wanting the court to make the decision you think needs to be made about the medical care of your child, right?
> **Dad**: That is right.
> **Attorney**: That is because you are an involved dad and do all you can for your son?

Dad: Right.

Attorney: Dad, do you exercise all the visitation the court orders say you can have with your son?

Dad: No, but that's because . . .

Attorney: Just answer the question yes or no.

Dad: No.

Attorney: In fact, you have missed every Thursday night visitation for the last two years, is that correct?

Dad: Yes.

Attorney: And when you had possession of your child, he was late for school over twenty times?

Dad: Correct.

There is nothing wrong with you if your work schedule does not allow for all the time you want with your children. Ask for a visitation plan that works for you, then exercise every bit of time you have.

Judge's Perspective
The Desperate Dad

Going through a divorce is one of the most stressful times of a person's life. You want to hold on to as much normalcy post-divorce as possible, especially when it comes to your kids. And your kids deserve to have as much normalcy as well. You want to spend as much time as you can with your kids as possible. When you are married you and your spouse share that time as it fits in to life's schedule. When Mom is at work, Dad gets to spend quality time with the kids. When

(Continued)

Dad is at work, Mom gets to do the things she wants to do with the kids. When a couple divorces it is much harder to balance everyone's schedule with the requirements of life.

Post-divorce you will not have the perfect schedule with your kids. If you choose to go to court instead of ADR the possibility of getting to see your kids on a schedule that works into your new life is even less likely.

I had a couple in my court litigating the issue of visitation schedules, meaning the parents could not agree on the time that each parent would spend with the children. The mom wanted a standard schedule where time with the kids would be based on alternating weekend. The father asked for a specific visitation schedule, an expanded weekend schedule. He proposed to pick up his son Thursday after school, return him to school the following Friday morning, pick him up after school Friday, and return him to school on Monday morning. His proposal was certainly a good option for a lot of couples and their kids.

The problem was, the father lived 70 miles from the child's school. While it might have seemed like an ideal schedule to Dad, it was an absolutely terrible schedule for the children. The children would have to wake up at 5 a.m. each day just to get in a car and ride for an hour and a half to school. The chances they would be late for school were high. After school on Thursday the children would get back in the car and have to drive another hour and a half to Dad's house which would interfere with homework time and other after schools activities. Friday morning would again come early at 5 a.m. and so on.

(Continued)

I pointed out to Dad how difficult this schedule would be for the children and for him. Once we went over the problems Dad acknowledged that he would not be able to exercise the visitation he had asked for. He knew it was absolutely impossible. Regardless, he was in court arguing for this schedule and paying his lawyer to argue for it as well. Why did he spend the money on legal fees to ask for something he could not do? Why didn't the lawyer catch this and point it out to him before taking his money?

The dad just wanted to spend as much time with his kids as he could. He was trying as hard as he could to make it work. I think going into court the schedule sounded good to him, but if he would have taken the time with his lawyer to go come up with a schedule that worked for him and the kids he would not have wasted his time and money on this issue.

I took a break from the trial and told the lawyers, Mom and Dad to go to a conference room and try to work on a schedule that worked for the parents and the children. About 40 minutes later they came into court with an agreement everyone was satisfied with. If the couple would have used an ADR method prior to coming into court I am confident everyone would have realized the parents needed a customized visitation schedule and would have reached an agreement. They could have avoided the time and expense of coming to court.

What about Supervised Visits?

Supervised visitation is an arrangement in which a parent is not allowed to be with the children unless accompanied by a designated adult. This person is usually a professional supervisor, although in some cases it is an agreed-upon family member. The supervisor monitors the visit to ensure the children's safety.

Some parents come to court asking for the other parent's visitation to be supervised. When asked why, they often say "He yells too much" or "She doesn't take care of them." With vague accusations like this, supervision is usually not necessary.

To justify supervised visits, there must be concrete evidence that the parent poses a real danger to the children. Examples of these situations include physical or emotional abuse, abandonment, drug or alcohol abuse, or a dangerous home environment. The goal is to protect the children while still allowing the affected parent to be a part of the children's lives.

In addition to the supervision requirement, the amount of visitation may be limited. Other significant restrictions may be placed on the parent as well. For example, a parent with history of drug abuse may be required to abstain from illegal drugs, attend a rehabilitation program, and submit to random drug tests. Parenting classes are often required as well.

Should these restrictions be placed on the parent forever? Not necessarily. Judges often use a stair-step approach, which you could use as well. In this approach, the amount of visitation is gradually increased. The parent must successfully comply with each step for three months before moving on to the next step. That means following all the terms of the agreement (such as receiving treatment and passing drug tests) and conducting appropriate, productive visits. Here are examples of the steps:

- Step 1: Begin with supervised visits for two hours every Saturday.
- Step 2: Increase supervised visits to four hours every Saturday.
- Step 3: Move from supervised to unsupervised visitation, but not overnight.
- Step 4: Add one unsupervised overnight visit per week, such as noon Saturday to noon Sunday.
- Step 5: If all continues to go well, move to a more standardized, "normal" schedule.

Of course, if the parent fails a drug test or stops going to drug rehabilitation or parenting classes, they would go back to Step 1 and start over.

If a parent poses a danger to children, you might think that the decision about visitation is better left to the court because the court will surely prevent access to the children. That is a reasonable thought. Understand that the court wants the children to have a solid, safe relationship with *both* parents. Parents with a history of drug addiction or other problems are given the chance to prove their ability to provide a safe environment for their children. If they pass the test, they will be allowed unsupervised visitation. Is it difficult to see this happen, even after they prove their sobriety? Absolutely. But children do not get to choose their parents. The parenting decision has already been made. Make the best of it for your children.

Plan the Exchanges

In addition to the visitation schedule, you will need to address the issue of who is responsible for picking up and dropping off the children for visitation and where this will take place. Normally, if one parent picks up the children at the beginning of their visitation, the other parent will pick them up at the conclusion of the visitation. If the parents live some distance apart from each other, they can agree to meet at a location midway between the two homes.

Since the parents are usually face-to-face during the exchanges, they sometimes think it's a perfect time to discuss issues they don't agree on. This isn't the case. The kids are there and they don't need to be in the middle of adult discussions, even if they aren't heated. If they do turn heated, the situation is even worse. If you need to talk with the other parent, find another time and place and do it privately.

Nor should you use a child as a messenger. If you have something to say to the other parent, send them a text or an email and leave the children out of it.

If you just can't stand the sight of your ex-spouse and simply can't keep your mouth shut, stay in the car. Just pull up to the drop-off location, say goodbye to your children, wish them a good time, let them get out, and drive away. Hopefully, this is not the situation you find yourself in. If it is, own it and do something about it for the sake of your children.

In some cases, one parent lives far enough away to require that the children travel by plane. Issues that the parents will need to address include who pays the airfare, what flight will the children be on, how much in advance should the flight schedule be confirmed, and what happens if the plane is delayed. Experienced family law attorneys, mediators, collaborative law attorneys, and arbitrators know the issues involving travel and will have creative ways to deal with them.

Prepare the Kids

You are doing your children a disservice if you do not prepare them for visitation. Children are very adaptable and will handle the situation better than you think—and probably better than you will. The way you approach the visitation and the attitude you have at the exchanges will set the tone for your children. The back-and-forth of visitation, with Mom and Dad going in and out of the children's day, is not ideal, but you must remember that this is the life of children of divorce. You are training the children on how life is going to be, so be positive and patient as all of you figure out how this is going to work out.

As the other parent's visitation period approaches, talk to your children in a positive way: "I am so excited for you. Your dad told me that he was taking all of you to the zoo!" You may be lying through your teeth about being excited, but do it for their sake. This is better than, "Well, your dad says he is taking you to the zoo *again*. That's not how I would spend the weekend with you." If you say that, right off the bat your children know that you are not happy about them spending time with their other parent. They may not figure it out now, but eventually they will see it for what it is. They will make up their own minds about their mom and dad. All you can control is your own relationship with your children. If you try to control the relationship your children have with their other parent, they will, as they get older, become resentful.

Finalize Your Plan

If you are using ADR to resolve your issues, you are already on a roll and understand the importance of working together. That is fantastic. Your relationship will ebb and flow, however.

So as you negotiate visitation, think of possible issues now, before they happen. As pessimistic as this may sound, think of the worst case scenario so you can plan around it.

Like the other terms of your divorce, your visitation agreement must be memorialized in writing. If you're settling your case using the IHOP method, you and your spouse can write the agreement together. If you have questions about what needs to be included or you need advice, find an attorney. If you went to Mediation without a lawyer, remember that you can hire an attorney on a limited-scope representation basis to review your agreement. If you went to Mediation with a lawyer or used Collaborative Law, your attorney will draft the necessary documents. Whatever ADR method you're using, always read the agreement before signing it. Make sure all the details are included and spelled out clearly.

Summing Up

Remember, if you cannot settle your divorce issues using ADR methods, ultimately a judge will decide the time you can spend with your children. A judge will be hard pressed to find the time to work out a visitation schedule that is perfect for your family, so do not leave it up to the judge. Work between yourselves or with a mediator or your attorneys to come up with a schedule that is right for your situation. Consider the uniqueness of your individual schedule, your spouse's, and those of your children to get something that will work. It will not be ideal. There will be sacrifices by everyone, but in the end, you will be in control and remain in control of the time each of you will have with your children.

14

Child Support

Each day of our lives we make deposits in the
memory banks of our children.

Charles R. Swindoll

Divorce is one of the leading causes of families going into
poverty in the United States. Mindful of this, legislatures
have passed child support statutes. These laws attempt to
ensure financial stability and a basic standard of living for
children of divorce, giving them a fighting chance for success.
If you and your spouse have a child under the age of majority
(depending on your state, between the ages of 18 and 21),
you will need to find out the child support laws in your state
and discuss this issue when resolving your divorce.

The Need for Child Support

Parents have an obligation to financially support their
children. Kids need a place to live, food to eat, clothes to wear,
and hundreds of other necessities. During their marriage,

parents use their joint resources to pay for these needs. If they divorce or separate, both of them are still responsible for providing for their children. Child support is a way for them to share this responsibility in a fair, equitable way.

The most typical situation involving child support occurs when the child primarily lives with one parent. The custodial parent is faced with everyday expenses such as making rent or mortgage payments, buying groceries and clothing, paying for medical care, and other costs of raising the child. The noncustodial parent has the obligation to supplement or share in those expenses in the form of child support payments.

In legal terms, the parent who is paying the child support is called the "obligor." The parent receiving child support is called the "obligee." The obligor makes child support payments to the obligee at regular intervals, usually monthly.

Unlike many other divorce issues, negotiating child support is often relatively straightforward. This chapter will explain the basic steps involved:

1. Research your state's laws and guidelines about child support.
2. Gather your financial information.
3. Apply the standard child support formula for your state.
4. If necessary, adjust the amount of child support to accommodate special needs.
5. Determine how child support will be paid.

Research Your State's Guidelines

Each state has specific child support guidelines that will guide your negotiations. Until you know the child support laws in your state, it's impossible to determine what amount of child support, if any, should be paid or received.

State guidelines can vary greatly. For example, in some states, child support is calculated as a percentage of the obligor's net income. Other states use both parents' income in their calculation.

Some states use child support to equalize the income of the parents. So if Father makes $75,000 a year and Mother makes $25,000, Father would pay close to $25,000 a year in child support. The theory is that the child benefits when both households (Mom's and Dad's) have an equal amount of the resources to care for the child. This theory really deviates from the general purpose of child support, but some states have adopted this as their model.

The amount of time each parent spends with the child may be a factor. In some states, if the custody arrangement gives both parents equal time with the child, then no child support is paid by either party. But in most states, equal parenting time does not eliminate the need to pay child support; the amount of payments may be adjusted to fit the situation.

State laws also affect how long child support must be paid. In some states, payments end when the child reaches the age of 18. Other states require payment until the child reaches 21.

Child support laws in individual states are distinctly different. So it is essential to understand the law in your state before negotiating this issue. The process will be a lot easier if you have the help of an attorney or mediator who knows how it all works. These professionals can explain the state guidelines and help you calculate the amount of payments. An attorney can also advise you (during or after negotiations) whether the figure you and your spouse agree on is fair. A mediator, however, is not allowed to give you legal advice.

Judge's Perspective
False Motivation

Child support is not litigated in court very often. However, some parents spend a considerable amount of money fighting over child support, and for all the wrong reasons.

One particular case comes to mind. The father spent a lot of time away from home because his job required frequent travel, but in the divorce trial, he asked to be designated as the custodial parent. When I asked how he was going to manage sole custody when he was away from home three days a week, he said his girlfriend (the one he'd had an affair with during the marriage) would take care of the child while he was on the road. When I asked him simple questions about his child, he was unable to give even basic answers.

If you think that I favor moms over dads when awarding child custody, you would be wrong. I certainly know that fathers, as well as mothers, can care for a child equally and that kids need both their parents. But in this particular case, I came to the conclusion that Dad really had no reasonable expectation of getting sole custody. Instead, he hoped that I would compromise by agreeing to give him 50-50 visitation with his child. He was under the mistaken belief that this would get him out of the requirement to pay child support.

The trial went on for a full day. I think each attorney charged over $30,000. In the end, Dad did get 50-50 possession time because he was a great father, but he was also ordered to pay child support in accordance with Texas

---

(Continued)

guidelines. All the money that was spent on legal fees could have gone to pay for the child's college or other expenses.

If Dad had used an ADR process, and had done so with reasonable and authentic goals in mind, it would have saved him, the mom, and the child the emotional and financial devastation of a child custody trial. The result would have been almost the same as if he had gone to court, but for much less money and stress.

Gather Financial Information

Once you have a basic understanding of the child custody laws in your state, the next step is to gather information about your financial resources. The most important factor is net income. Your state guidelines should explain how to calculate this. In some states, you'll need to know the net income of each parent. Others require only the net income of the parent who is going to pay child support.

Depending on your state, you may also need other financial information. For example, if you live in Florida, you'll need to know the monthly amount that each parent pays for daycare and for medical, dental, and vision insurance.

In addition to financial data, you may need other information. The number of children you have is obviously important. Some states take other factors into account, such as whether either spouse is receiving spousal or child support from a previous marriage.

Apply the State Formula

Once you have all the required information, you can plug it into the standard child support formula for your state. Some websites offer charts or online calculators for figuring child support. If you prefer, you can let your attorney or mediator make the calculation.

The result will tell you the standard amount of child support that state guidelines recommend for your situation. However, the standard formula may not take all your individual needs into account. In the next step, you will make adjustments to accommodate those needs.

Adjust for Special Situations

State child support guidelines are just that—guidelines. They are designed to meet the needs of typical cases. But if your case isn't typical, the recommended amount of child support may not be enough. Each state has a list of factors to consider when determining whether additional child support is needed which can be used to help guide discussions and negotiation during ADR. Consulting this list can help you negotiate a payment amount that is more appropriate for your situation.

For example, a child with substantial health problems may require special health equipment in the home. Or a child may have substantial educational needs that require one-on-one tutoring or a specialized private school. If you are in a situation like this, you and your spouse will need to figure out what these extra expenses are and how they should be accounted for when calculating child support in your state.

On the other hand, in some cases the amount of child support can be lower than the state guidelines suggest. For instance, the child may have a trust fund or other substantial source of income. The obligor may be supporting elderly parents and have fewer resources available for child support. Again, consult the list of factors that your state has identified.

Determine the Payment Method

In addition to the amount of child support, you and your spouse will have to agree on how it will be paid. The choice of payment method is important because it needs to protect both sides. Every time child support is paid, it's essential to have a record of how much was paid and when. This confirms that payments are being made in accordance with the agreement.

Never agree that the payment will be made in cash. With cash there is no official record. This puts everyone at a disadvantage when trying to prove that the payment was or was not made.

Some states have a child support agency where all child support payments have to be made. If your state allows for direct payments, electronic bank transfers are probably the best way to ensure a proper record of the transaction. Another option is to write a check or money order and deposit it to a bank account of the parent receiving child support. Figure out the method that works the best for your situation while protecting everyone.

Never allow the child to be the go-between in delivering child support payments. Although this sounds obvious, it does happen. Imagine you're the child in this situation. When you return home after visiting Dad or Mom, you walk in the door and the first thing you hear is, "Did you get the child support check?" This isn't healthy or helpful.

What If Child Support Isn't Paid?

The reason why everyone wants a record of the child support payment is simple: not paying child support can have serious consequences. The Child Support Agreement will be put into a court order that is signed by a judge. Failure to follow the orders of the court can result in the offending party being held in contempt of court. This can result in a fine or even jail.

In addition to the contempt of court charge, other measures can be taken against those who do not pay child support. The state can revoke or suspend their driver's license or other state-issued licenses, such as a real estate license, law license, plumber's license, and so on. The federal government can seize their tax refunds and use them to pay child support.

Needless to say, if you have agreed, or been ordered, to pay child support, take this obligation seriously. Make the payments in full and on time. Even when you and your ex-spouse are getting along, make sure there is a record of your payments. There may be a time where the tide changes and you find yourself having to defend yourself. For most parents this advice is obvious, but there are still some who do not take the support of their child seriously. Do not be one of those parents.

If you are a parent who is not receiving your child support you can file legal papers to have the court enforce the child support order. In some states, there is a government agency who is responsible for helping parents in this situation get their child support paid. If you need to go to court to force your ex to pay child support you will probably need to hire an attorney. Enforcing a child support order requires very specific paperwork and evidence that would be difficult for you to prepare and gather on your own. Once in the courtroom the judge will require very specific testimony and records to prove that child support has not been paid. The attorney will know what needs to be filed and proven to get you your child support. You may be thinking: "I do not have the money to pay for an attorney." That is understandable. If you win in court, it is highly likely that the judge will require your ex-spouse to pay your attorney's fees in addition to the child support you are owed. Your children deserve their child support and the financial burden of raising your children should not fall solely on you. Go get your child support.

Summing Up

Child support is generally straightforward. It is what it is. The key to determining the payment of child support is having all the financial information needed to put it to your state's calculation. While the time each parent spends with the child does figure into the calculation of child support, it rarely stops the child support obligation all together. Whether you are paying or receiving child support, remember that child support is to go towards the support of the child.

Once payment of child support is established the obligor will face severe consequences if not paid.

Child support provides yet another example of why ADR is important in resolving your disputes. You and your spouse are the ones who best understand your children's needs. You know the financial resources available to you better than anyone. You have it within yourselves to figure out the solution best suited for each of you and—most importantly—your children.

Once child support is ordered to be paid, it should be paid. If you are not getting the court ordered child support, then take the legal steps necessary to get your ex-spouse to pay it.

Part Four

MAKING IT
LEGAL

15

Hiring an Attorney

An attorney is one who defends you at the risk
of your pocketbook, reputation, and life.
Eugene E. Brussell

We have all seen them on TV: the big-time, intimidating
lawyers in their posh offices with massive wooden tables and
conference rooms the size of our houses, but that is just television. Most lawyers, especially those who practice family
law, are down-to-earth folks who provide a service to those in
need of a divorce. They are generally very approachable and
are truly there to help.

No matter what approach you take to getting a divorce—
the IHOP method, Mediation, Collaborative Law, Arbitration, or court litigation—lawyers are an essential part of the
process. This chapter will help you find a lawyer who fits your
needs and expectations.

Options for Hiring an Attorney

When you're getting a divorce, you have several options when it comes to hiring an attorney. You can choose not to have an attorney; you can bring in an attorney to do certain tasks; or you can hire an attorney to handle your entire case.

Represent Yourself

If you choose the IHOP method or Mediation, you and your spouse have the option to finalize the divorce between yourselves, without the help of an attorney. You are certainly entitled to represent yourself in any legal proceeding, including divorce. Most counties or states have law libraries that can provide you with the forms you need to fill out and file with the court to get a divorce. The law libraries have instruction sheets that explain the who, what, when, why, and how of getting a divorce.

However, if you go it alone, you do so at your own risk. This simply means that while you have the right to represent yourself, you have to decide if that's a good idea. If you have little to no marital property and no kids, representing yourself might be a viable option. If you have a fair amount of marital property and a child or children, you are on shakier ground. And if you have a lot of property and complicated child custody or child support issues, you are probably better off hiring an attorney. The forms you get from the law library can tell you how to file for divorce, but they cannot protect your interests or give you legal advice. For that, you need a lawyer.

Limited-Scope Representation

Suppose you are remodeling your house. You are pretty handy and can do a lot of the work yourself, which will save money. However, you know your limitations. You are not comfortable with handling the electrical work or the plumbing. For those specific tasks, you decide to hire qualified professionals.

This is the essence of Limited-Scope Representation. You hire an attorney to do specified tasks at one or more stages of the divorce process. The lawyer handles some aspects of your case and you handle the rest.

Limited-Scope Representation reduces costs while ensuring that your legal rights are protected. The attorney can provide whatever type of legal assistance you ask for: explaining your legal options, evaluating proposals, reviewing agreements, drafting the Final Decree/Order, or other tasks. You maintain control of the process, bringing in the attorney as needed. Your spouse can hire an attorney on a Limited-Scope Representation basis as well.

There are many examples of how you could use Limited-Scope Representation. Here are a few:

- You consult a lawyer at the beginning of your case to get legal information, advice, and strategies to use later as you need them.
- You hire an attorney to represent you on specific issues in your case, such as child support or child custody.
- You work with your spouse using the IHOP method, then hire an attorney to review your agreement and draft the final order that will be presented to the court.
- You consult a lawyer about complex legal questions,

such as whether your spouse is entitled to any interest in a piece of property you inherited.

- You hire a lawyer to represent you during mediation sessions.
- You go to Mediation without a lawyer, but have an attorney review the final agreement before you sign it.

Limited-Scope Representation does have disadvantages. Your attorney will not have a full picture of all the issues in your divorce and how they are interrelated. If you inadvertently leave out an important piece of information, the attorney may give you the wrong advice. Weigh these drawbacks against the benefits of Limited-Scope Representation before deciding whether it's right for you.

The concept of Limited-Scope Representation is new to most attorneys. They are accustomed to being hired to represent clients through the entire divorce process, from beginning to end. But with the popularization of ADR, many attorneys are realizing there's another niche for clients who can benefit from legal advice, but want to limit their costs. You can find lawyers familiar with Limited-Scope Representation at www.divorceinpeace.com.

Full Representation

The third option is to have an attorney handle all the legal matters in your case, from the time you decide to file for divorce until it's final. This is called Full Representation.

When a couple gets a divorce through a court trial, Full Representation is a given. In that situation, the lawyers are brought in at the very beginning. When you use ADR, however, you have the flexibility to decide on Full Representation at any point in the process. For example, you and your spouse could try the IHOP method first, working through your issues together without lawyers. But if you found IHOP was not working, you would have the option of hiring an attorney to fully represent you through the rest of the divorce. Full Representation is built into Collaborative Law and Arbitration. It can also be used with Mediation, if you wish.

If you have a high net worth or are dealing with complicated issues in your divorce, you may want Full Representation no matter which ADR process you use.

At whatever point Full Representation begins, the attorney assumes all the legal aspects of your case. He or she will handle everything from the formal discovery process to presenting your final divorce decree to the judge. The only way to maintain control of your entire divorce, with an attorney or not, is to use an ADR process. Remember, you are trying to Divorce in Peace. Make sure you hold the attorney accountable to your goals and wishes.

Your Needs

Before you look for an attorney, think about your needs and goals. Are you leaning toward a particular ADR method? What do you want the attorney to accomplish for you? Do you want Limited-Scope Representation or Full Representation? With your needs firmly in mind, you will be better able to narrow down your search and make your expectations clear to the attorneys you talk with.

The Search Process

No matter where you live, you can probably find a wide selection of attorneys in your area who handle divorce cases. They may be called divorce attorneys, matrimonial attorneys, or family law attorneys. For instance, you can go to your state's Bar Association website to find attorneys in your area.

The challenge, however, is finding a lawyer who will help you Divorce in Peace. You want an attorney who understands ADR processes and their importance in preserving the family's emotional and financial health. The last thing you want is a lawyer who immediately tells you how much better you could do by going to court—and in the next breath, asks for a large fee to litigate your case.

There are several ways to find attorneys who are familiar with the low-stress methods of dissolving a marriage. We recommend you start by visiting www.divorceinpeace.com. Lawyers who have pledged to the basic tenets and concepts in this book are listed there. It is our mission to find attorneys who believe in ADR and make them available to clients who want to Divorce in Peace.

Personal recommendations are another option. You could talk to friends, neighbors, and work associates who have gone through a divorce themselves, especially if they have used any of the ADR methods. They may have either good or not so good things to say about their attorney or the attorney who represented their spouse. If you know any attorneys or judges, you might ask them which lawyer they would recommend for a divorce using your chosen ADR method and why.

Once you have a list of candidates do some research to learn more. For instance, on most law firms' websites you can find information about the background and experience of their attorneys, references to ADR methods—such as Collaborative Divorce, and perhaps taste a flavor for their overall philosophy. If you have specific questions—whether a particular attorney is open to Limited-Scope Representation or has experience with Collaborative Law—you can call the law firm and ask.

If your situation is very contentious, you may want a lawyer who has extensive experience in both ADR and litigation. An attorney with this background can walk you competently and professionally through all the ADR methods. If ADR doesn't result in an agreement, the attorney will have enough experience to represent you in court. Of course, the more experience attorneys have, the more they charge.

You may want to find out whether the attorneys you are considering are board certified. Board certification recognizes attorneys who have taken extensive continuing legal education classes in their specialty area and who have passed an extensive exam. Certification is a voluntary process, not a requirement. There are certainly good lawyers who are not board certified. Most of the time, board certified attorneys charge more for their time.

The Initial Consultation

So you've done your research and found at least one attorney who sounds promising. Is your search finished? Not quite. The only sure-fire way to confirm you have found the right professional is to interview the attorney and ask questions that will help you make a decision.

Usually, the way to arrange this is by setting up an initial consultation. When you make the appointment, find out whether the attorney will charge a fee for this consultation. Some do, while others do not. This is not a reflection of the attorney's legal ability or need for clients. It is simply a preference that varies from attorney to attorney.

During your initial consultation, remember the attorney

is interviewing for the job. Even though lawyers can be intimidating and often talk in what seems to be a different language, you are the boss. Here are some suggestions for what to discuss during the initial consultation:

Your needs and expectations. Let the attorney know what you are looking for. Explain which ADR method you are considering, the type of services you want, and whether you want Limited-Scope Representation or Full Representation. For example, you might say, "We have drafted our own divorce agreement and are hiring a lawyer to review it," or "We plan to get a divorce using Collaborative Law, and I need an attorney to represent me." During the rest of the consultation, try to determine how well the lawyer meets the personal and legal needs you have identified.

ADR experience. Ask how many cases the attorney has settled using ADR versus going to trial; and how much experience the attorney has in the method you are interested in. Ask for the attorney's opinion about the preferred method and how he or she would approach the process. Discuss which method might be best for your situation and why, and how the lawyer would approach the case. You can then decide if you are comfortable with his or her approach to your specific issues.

Experience with the local court system. One of the most advantageous aspects of an attorney's background is whether or not he or she is familiar with the court system and judges in the jurisdiction where your case is or will be filed. An attorney who knows the local court system and the judges will help you in evaluating your case and determining whether your negotiation position is reasonable in your area.

Specific issues in your case. Tell the attorney about any aspects of your case that you are especially concerned about, such as disputes over property division or child custody. Ask about the attorney's experience in these areas. While all family law attorneys work with these issues, some may be especially skilled in resolving certain types of disputes. Also ask the attorney to explain the law on these issues and the probable outcome if you took your case to court.

Fees. The commodity attorneys sell is their time. They bill by the hour or fraction of an hour. This hourly billing will also apply to their staff, mainly legal assistants. Find out the hourly rates. You will also be billed for expenses such as filing fees, deposition fees, subpoena fees, copying fees, long distance phone calls, postage, delivery fees, and the costs of bringing in experts. Ask the attorney to estimate the total cost of your case.

Although everyone wants to find the best possible attorney, your choices may be limited by the amount of money you can afford to spend. Hourly rates vary widely from town to town and from attorney to attorney. Legal assistants' rates can range from $80 to $250 an hour, and attorneys' rates can range from $150 to $1000 an hour or more. While you may be tempted to shell out the big bucks because "my kids are worth it" or "I would spend everything I have to keep the house," this attitude is not very realistic. While you might be able to afford an expensive attorney at the beginning of your case, if you run out of money your attorney will not, in all likelihood, continue representing you. You could end up being left out in the cold with no attorney at all. Choose an attorney you can afford from beginning to end, you will be better off.

Retainer Agreement and Billing

If you are satisfied with the interview and decide to hire the attorney, you will be required to sign a Retainer Agreement and pay an initial retainer. A retainer is a fee paid in advance to the law firm to secure the services of the attorney. Why does the firm need a retainer? First, it guarantees payment for the time used on your behalf. Second, the firm will use that money to pay for out-of-pocket expenses that will come up almost immediately, such as filing fees.

The retainer will be placed in a separate account, often referred to as a Client Trust Fund. The money stays there until the firm has earned fees by working on your case. Typically, each month the firm will send you a bill that details the tasks that have been done, the personnel who did the work, the time spent on each task, and the cost. Everything that has been done in your case is included: phone calls, emails, letters, drafting court documents, inter-office conferences, hearings, settlement conferences, and so on. Expenses are included as well. The amount of the bill will be deducted from your retainer. Most attorneys will ask that you maintain a certain balance in your account. Therefore, as the retainer is used up, you will periodically need to make additional payments.

Whether any unused portion of the retainer is refundable will depend on the attorney or the firm. Some firms refund the entire unused amount. Others refund a portion of it, while still others won't refund any of the retainer.

The fees, billing method, refund policy, and other details should be outlined in the Retainer Agreement. Read this document carefully before you sign it, and ask questions if you don't understand all the terms.

Judge's Perspective
Choose Your Attorney Carefully

Most attorneys know how to effectively represent their clients in a cost-effective way. As with any profession, there are good attorneys and there are bad attorneys. A bad attorney can take advantage of the emotions surrounding a divorce, turn minor disagreements into major conflicts, create conflict that doesn't exist, and run up unnecessary legal fees.

In one case that came before me, the couple had over $500,000 in a savings account. My fear was that the lawyers would fight every issue and use this savings account to pay for it. I was right. Once the money was all used up, the lawyers were gone and their clients, now unrepresented, were left to pick up the pieces. Attorney's fees had exceeded $700,000.

To a significant degree, the fault lies with the couple. If they could not agree on anything, their lawyers had no choice but to fight for their clients. The blame has to be partly borne by the lawyers. Their legal maneuvers were unnecessary; they fought on even the most basic legal issues. I could tell one attorney in particular was "milking the file," meaning he was causing unnecessary conflict to make more money.

My point is, hiring an attorney is not a decision to be taken lightly. The lawyer you choose will set the tone for your divorce from the moment he or she is hired. Unfortunately, there are a few lawyers who will capitalize on your misfortune. Use what you have learned in this book

---

(Continued)

to avoid them. Ask a lot of questions at the initial consultation. Ask around your community about the reputation of the attorney. If you have any doubts at all, get a second opinion.

Always understand that you are the boss. If you have questions, ask them. If you are unhappy, say so. And if the case is not being handled the way you want, fire the attorney.

The good news is that the overwhelming majority of attorneys who practice in the area of divorce do so because they have a passion for people and families. They are mindful of the pitfalls of divorce and the damage a highly contentious divorce can have on families, especially kids. Find an attorney like this and you have found someone special who will guide you through the troubled waters of your divorce.

Working with Your Lawyer

Once you have hired an attorney, the next steps depend on what you have asked the attorney to do and which ADR method you are using.

For example, suppose you hire an attorney on a Limited-Scope Representation basis to review an agreement you have entered into with your spouse. If you brought the agreement with you, some attorneys may be willing to review it during the initial consultation. Others may want time to read it and will ask you to make a follow-up appointment.

If you have hired your attorney to represent you in Mediation, Collaborative Law, or Arbitration, you will probably be given a list of documents and information to gather for their review. This might include information about your bank accounts, mortgage, retirement plan, and other financial records. In addition, the attorney will ask you to prepare an Inventory and Appraisement, I&A, (see Appendix M), which will detail the assets and debts acquired during the marriage as well as any separate property that will be claimed. These documents and others will help the attorney evaluate your case and establish a strategy to move forward.

Summing Up

The key in hiring any person who provides professional services is your confidence in that person. If you do not get a confident feeling from a lawyer you consult with, find another one. The lawyer you hire and trust will help you make some of the biggest decisions for you and your family. Find one you are comfortable with.

16

Finalizing the Divorce

Everyone goes through adversity in life, but
what matters is how you learn from it.

Lou Holtz

At some point, we hope you will have successfully completed
one of the ADR processes outlined in this book. Depending
on the method you used, you may have already come up with
a written agreement using IHOP, a signed Letter of Understanding, or a Mediated Settlement Agreement. These papers
will incorporate all the agreements you've reached during the
course of your negotiations. If you go to Arbitration, you will
have a decision from the arbitrator; if you go to court, you
will have the judge's ruling. You are almost there. Just a few
more steps are needed in order to finalize your divorce.

Preparing Your Paperwork

To be officially married, you had to have a Certificate of
Marriage. To be officially divorced, you have to have an order

signed by a judge—a Final Decree/Order. The Final Decree/ Order will need to incorporate all the agreements you've reached, plus specific legal language required in divorce decrees by your state. In legal jargon, a decree is an enforceable order based on legal authority. That simply means after the judge signs the decree, both you and your former spouse will be legally bound to follow the terms spelled out in the decree. You will be officially divorced.

Before you go to court, the Final Decree/Order will need to be prepared so it is ready for the judge's signature. If you used a lawyer throughout the divorce process, he or she will draft the Final Decree/Order and any other paperwork you need. Otherwise, you can hire a lawyer on a Limited-Scope Representation basis to finalize your documents. If you prefer a do-it-yourself approach, you can find forms for a Final Decree/ Order at a law library or online. No matter how your decree is prepared, make sure it includes every one of the provisions you and your spouse have agreed to and both of your signatures.

In addition to the Final Decree/Order, you will need to gather other documents that will help conclude the divorce. These might include:

- Documents transferring the titles of the home, cars, or other property.
- A wage withholding order—allowing child support to be taken out of the paycheck of the person paying child support.
- A Qualified Domestic Relations Order (QDRO). This is required by employer-sponsored pension or retirement plans in order to divide an account upon divorce.

Your attorney or other sources can help you determine

what documents you need in your case. Make sure you have all the documents you need so you only have to make one trip to the courthouse.

Going to Court

Now that all your paperwork is in order, the next step is to go to court for a Prove Up; it sounds scarier than it is.

The Prove Up is a hearing before a judge. It must take place at the same court where you filed for divorce. In most states, only one of the spouses needs to be present. Check the requirements in your state. Your attorney may be present as well.

At the Prove Up, you will be given an oath and will have to answer certain questions about your marriage and divorce. Typical questions are:

- When did you get married?
- When did you separate?
- How long did you live in the state before filing for divorce?
- Were any children born or adopted during the marriage?
- Have you reach agreements about custody? Are those agreement in the best interest of the child?
- Did you acquire property during the marriage? Did you reach an agreement about how to divide the property?
- Do you want a name change?
- Do you want the court to grant the divorce?

This is not an adversarial process; you are not cross-examined by the judge or a lawyer. This process ensures the court has jurisdiction over you and your kids and that there is really an agreement which resolves all the issues in the divorce.

At the conclusion of your testimony, the court will approve your agreement and grant you a divorce. The judge will sign your Final Decree/Order and any other legal papers that need to be signed, like title transfers and wage withholding orders. You will be given a copy of the Final Decree/Order to take with you for your records, or the Court Clerk's office will make it available online. You may be required to provide copies of your Final Decree/Order to certain organizations, such as your bank or your child's school, that need to know the terms of your divorce.

Judge's Perspective
The End of this Chapter in Life

You might think when couples come to finalize their divorce they would be relieved, and maybe even happy, that they have finally finished the divorce process. Often this is true. On the other hand, sometimes both parties are crying. I assume their tears come from the realization their dreams of living happily-ever-after together are over. I often wonder whether, at some point, they wanted to stop the divorce but didn't know how. Or after the legal fees were spent and hurtful words were exchanged they couldn't turn back.

The tears may be just an expression of relief that this chapter of their life is over. Whatever the reason for the emotions and tears, it's a window into the true feelings of these individuals.

(Continued)

So before you go down the divorce road, make sure realize what you are doing and why. Think about what life will be like after the divorce, and whether it really is what you want to do. Try everything you possibly can to avoid divorce so 10 years down the road, when you look in the mirror and at your kids, you will know you did everything you could to keep your marriage and family together.

If you are convinced a divorced life is better for you than your married life, approach the divorce with a level head and a steady heart. Pick an ADR method in this book that best fits your situation. ADR only works when people are willing to compromise. I am not telling you to throw in the towel and give up everything in hopes of a peaceful divorce. I am asking you to make solid, reasonable and thoughtful efforts to solve your divorce issues rather than be overcome by emotions and a desire to hurt the other person. As you have learned, this is self-destructive, both emotionally and financially.

And when all is said and done, I hope you can close this chapter of your life knowing other doors will open. Use what you have learned in this past relationship to make your future relationships stronger. And, if you have kids, take the time to hug and love on your kids.

Sometimes divorce is the necessary step in your journey towards happiness. We hope that if you divorce, you will Divorce in Peace.

Amending the Decree

If you don't have any kids and the divorce is all about the property division, you cannot modify the final decree. If you do have children and if for some reason down the road the agreements you have made about are not working, you can amend the decree. We aren't talking about situations where you have "buyer's remorse"—that is, you are upset about the agreement you reached. We are talking about real problems that cause the arrangements in the decree to no longer be in the child's best interest.

If this happens—and we hope it does not—you can file a Motion to Modify and seek to amend the decree. The negotiation process would start all over. We hope that you would "modify in peace" using the ADR methods and the skills you learned in this book, to arrive at an agreement that better meets your children's needs.

Summing Up

If you make it through the divorce process without the court having to make decisions about your finances or kids, congratulations! First and foremost, you should be congratulated for maintaining control of the decisions regarding your finances and children. You have also saved yourself from the emotional devastation that accompanies contentious divorces, saved a lot of money, helped your kids be protected from conflict, and kept your personal matters out of the public sphere of the courtroom. Hopefully, you also learned how to communicate a little better with your ex-spouse.

Now, you will have to learn to live life after divorce. Continue to focus on yourself and your children. Take some of the positive lessons you have learned through this process and use them to resolve other disputes that may arise.

After the divorce, live life to the fullest. Look forward, not backwards. Take what you learned in your previous relationship, find out where you went wrong, and fix it. In your next relationship—and yes, there will be another relationship—go slow and wait years to remarry.

And if you get a call from your best friend, asking for the meanest, nastiest divorce lawyer you know so they can take their lying, cheating spouse to the cleaners, do this person a huge favor. Recommend that your friend take a deep breath and seek a Divorce in Peace.

Thank you for taking the time to learn how to Divorce in Peace. We hope you find peace in your divorce and in everything you do.

APPENDICES

Appendix A
Divorce in Peace Attorney Pledge

I UNDERSTAND divorce or disputes involving children can be emotionally and financially devastating to all involved;

I UNDERSTAND going to court to resolve such conflicts add to the emotional and financial stress of an already stressful situation;

I UNDERSTAND going to court to resolve such conflicts takes the power over family decisions away from husbands and wives or fathers and mothers and gives it to a judge;

I UNDERSTAND the more the parties argue over aspects of the divorce the more money it costs;

I UNDERSTAND there are many other ways to resolve the issues involving divorce and/or child custody without going to court including mediation, collaborative law and arbitration. I am familiar with and support these alternatives to court;

I UNDERSTAND you are putting your trust in me to resolve your divorce and/or child custody dispute in a manner consistent with my legal obligations but being ever mindful of the cost of continuing legal battles.

AS A RESULT OF THE FOREGOING,

I PLEDGE to attempt to settle your divorce in a non-adversarial manner to minimize the emotional and financial impact of the case on you;

I PLEDGE to efficiently and economically settle your divorce or child custody case by attempting mediation, collaborative law or arbitration;

I PLEDGE to not pursue disputes where the cost is greater than the benefit to you and your family;

I PLEDGE to fulfill my legal obligation to you while embracing the principles set forth in *Divorce in Peace.*

Appendix B
Comparison of ADR Methods
and Court Trial

IHOP (Informal Healthy Opportunity for Peace)

Voluntary negotiation between spouses without the use of lawyers or mediators; based on ground rules and an agenda to resolve issues

Pluses (+)	Minuses (-)
Private process; no court transcripts	Requires discipline and rigid adherence to ground rules
You and your spouse have total control	Both spouses must leave their rants at home and focus on the issues: (1) dividing assets and (2) providing for the children
Least expensive way to avoid a warring divorce; preserves assets for your, your spouse's, and your children's future	Doesn't work if there is family violence or other illegal conduct by one or both spouses

Pluses (+)	Minuses (-)
If you learn to communicate about issues now, you can use the techniques to resolve post-divorce disputes	
If you can make IHOP work, you'll probably still be on speaking terms with your spouse after the divorce; better for your mental and financial health and that of your children and spouse	
Costs nothing to try; other options still open if you can't agree	

Appendix C
Private Mediation

Voluntary negotiation between parties facilitated by a third party neutral (mediator) aimed at reaching a framework of the agreement before bringing lawyers into the process

Pluses (+)	Minuses (-)
Faster resolution than going to court	Doesn't work if parties' relationship is too impaired to meet in the same room with the mediator to discuss issues
Private way to reach agreement rather than addressing issues in a public courtroom	Doesn't work unless both parties are candid about the extent of marital assets and debts
Parties choose mediator versus randomly assigned judge in public court	Cost of joint experts (if needed) can be high, but less than if the couple goes to court, each hiring their own adversarial, competing experts
Parties control outcome, not the court; more likely to comply with an agreement you develop	Settlement agreement binding once signed; parties should consult lawyer before signing

Pluses (+)	Minuses (-)
Techniques learned in private mediation can be used to resolve post-divorce disputes	
Less legal fees than court or regular mediation where lawyers are involved in hammering out the agreement	
If hired, cost of joint experts to address specific concerns will be less than court where each side hires their own competing, adversarial experts	

Appendix D
Mediation

Court-ordered or voluntary negotiation process between parties facilitated by a third party neutral (mediator) meeting with the parties and their lawyers (if retained) to reach a binding settlement agreement

Pluses (+)	Minuses (-)
Faster resolution than going to court	More legal fees than private mediation since each party's lawyer generally involved throughout the process
Private way to reach agreement rather than addressing issues in a public courtroom	Settlement agreement is binding once parties sign; court intervention not an option
If parties can't reach a mediated settlement and go to court, what happened during mediation may not be used in the court trial	Doesn't work if one spouse is trying to prevent a divorce and drags out the negotiations for as long as possible or if one spouse is too angry to focus on solutions to the issues

Pluses (+)	Minuses (-)
Parties choose mediator versus randomly assigned judge in public court	Doesn't work if one party tries to hide or transfer marital assets or debts
Parties control outcome, not the court; more likely to comply with an agreement you develop	
Techniques learned in mediation can be used to resolve future disputes	
Flexible process allowing parties to be in separate rooms represented by their own lawyer	
If hired, cost of joint experts to address specific concerns will be less than court where each side hires their own competing, adversarial experts	

Appendix E
Collaborative Law

ADR process in which the spouses and their lawyers (specifically trained in collaborative law) work together in good faith to resolve the issues involved in the divorce without court intervention

Pluses (+)	Minuses (-)
Parties control outcome, not the court	Doesn't work unless both parties are candid about the extent of marital assets and debts
Parties have the support of a lawyer throughout the process whose role is to ensure a cooperative approach to coming up with a mutually satisfying settlement of the issues	If any party or lawyer threatens or tries to use the court during the process, the collaborative lawyers must immediately withdraw, and parties incur cost of starting over with new lawyers for litigation
Saves financial and emotional resources; often less expensive than litigation	
Allows creativity to customize the agreement that isn't possible within the one-size-fits-all rule of law the court must follow	

Pluses (+)	Minuses (−)
Parties agree to confidentiality in the collaborative agreement; can't use anything said during collaborative process in trial unless parties agree	
Parties can retain a neutral expert without fear that the expert could later be called to testify against either spouse if the case ultimately goes to trial	

Appendix F
Arbitration

Voluntary, private process of hiring an arbitrator, or private judge, to make final decisions in a divorce case in a more informal hearing; binding arbitration generally used but can also be nonbinding

Pluses (+)	Minuses (-)
Allows for a judge in high conflict cases to make decisions without the long resolution time of the public court system	Parties must pay for arbitrator, court reporter, and all other case expenses compared with the public system where the State (taxpayer) pays these costs
Generally less expensive than public court trial	May have hearing without complete discovery since arbitrator, unlike a judge, can make a decision based on incomplete evidence if evidenced is deemed conclusive
Parties choose arbitrator versus randomly assigned judge in public court	Arbitrator makes the final decision, so parties don't control the outcome; arbitrator may not explain reasoning for the final decision in the opinion and order

Pluses (+)	Minuses (-)
More informal hearing and less stressful than public court proceedings	Can't appeal the final decision (but an advantage if you like the final decision)
Process emphasizes cooperation and maintaining good future relations	
Private process; information is confidential	
Since binding arbitration order is final, there is no cost or time spent on appeals; in nonbinding arbitration, if you don't like the decision, you can go to trial	

Appendix G
Court Trial

Using the public court system to make final decisions about your divorce

Pluses (+)	Minuses (-)
Courts can order and enforce protective orders in cases of domestic violence	Courts are crowded, and it could take several years to hear your case
Offers a last resort to have final decisions made and legally enforced if nothing else works	Litigation is stressful, time consuming, and expensive
	A party may try to use the courts to punish their spouse or as a public forum to complain about their spouse, wasting financial resources that would be better spent on the children's and spouses' future

Pluses (+)	Minuses (-)
	You give up control over the outcome to a stranger—a judge you don't select who is charged with applying the rule of law whether or not it's best in your situation
	Adversarial nature of court system likely to impair future relations with your spouse to resolve post-divorce disputes about children, alimony, etc.
	Discovery (gathering information for trial) is subject to strict rules and can be expensive, stressful, and time consuming

Appendix H
Family Law Court System Flowchart

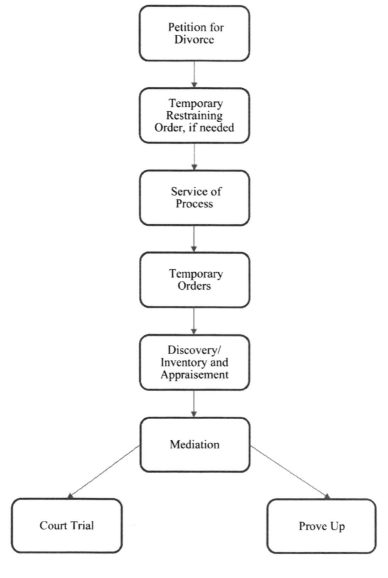

Appendix I
Checklist of Issues to Be Resolved

PROPERTY DIVISION

Real Property
A. House
  1. Who wants/gets/can afford it
  2. How much is it worth
  3. Mortgage balance/Home equity
  4. Mortgage tax write-offs
  5. Tax consequences of transfer or sale
  6. Sell it? If so, how and for how much
  7. Realtor
  8. Repair costs
  9. How to get stuff out
  10. Refinance
B. Other Real Property

Personal Property
A. Automobiles/Other Vehicles
B. Household Furniture
C. Collectibles
D. Equipment

Financial Assets
A. Retirement accounts/Pension Plans
B. Stocks, bonds, money market accounts
C. Bank Accounts

D. Life Insurance

E. Airline/Hotel miles

Debts

A. Credit cards, personal loans

B. Joint debts, who is responsible

C. Cars

Income Tax

A. Filing

B. Refunds

C. Taxes owed

D. File jointly or separately

CHILD ISSUES

A. Parenting Plan
    1. Time with each parent
    2. Weekdays
    3. Weekends
    4. Summer
    5. Holidays

B. Geographical Restriction
    1. Parent restricted from moving with child

C. Parental Decision Making (joint, separate, by agreement0
    1. Medical/Dental care
    2. Educational
    3. Athletics/Extracurricular
    4. Religious

D. Other Rules for Parents (Injunctions)
    1. Alcohol around kids
    2. Dangerous activities

3. Certain individuals not allowed around kids
4. No spending night with a romantic other while in possession of kids

E. Child Support
1. Guideline payment or reason to deviate from guideline
2. Amount/date of payment
3. Secured by life insurance
4. Special Needs Child

F. College Expenses

G. Automobile expenses for kids

H. Medical Insurance/Expenses
1. Who carries
2. Amounts not covered
3. Orthodontics, vision
4. Mental issues

I. Spousal Support
1. Part of property division
2. Taxable income to one spouse
3. How much per month
4. How long are payments

Appendix J
Collaborative Law Participation Sample Agreement

Purpose

John Smith and Mary Smith (the "parties") have chosen to use the principles of collaborative law to settle the issues of their divorce in a non-adversarial manner. John Smith has retained (Attorney Name) and Mary Smith has retained (Attorney Name) as collaborative attorneys to assist them in reaching this goal. We, the parties and their attorneys, acknowledge that the essence of collaborative law is the shared belief of the participants that, in typical family law matters, it is in the best interests of parties and their families to commit themselves to avoiding litigation.

We therefore adopt this conflict resolution process, which does not rely on court-imposed resolutions but relies instead on an atmosphere of honesty, cooperation, integrity, and professionalism geared toward the future well-being of the family. Our goal is to minimize, if not eliminate, the negative economic, social, and emotional consequences of protracted litigation to the parties and their families. We commit ourselves to the collaborative law process and agree to seek a better way to resolve our differences justly and equitably.

Communication

We agree to effectively and honestly communicate with each other with the goal of efficiently and economically settling the terms of the dissolution of the marriage. We agree that all written and oral communications between us will be respectful and constructive and that we will not make accusations or claims not based in fact. We agree to give full, honest, and open disclosure of all information, whether requested or not.

We agree that settlement meetings will be focused on economic and parenting issues and the constructive resolution of those issues. We agree not to engage in unnecessary discussions of past events.

All conversations during the collaborative process are in the nature of settlement negotiations. Therefore, we agree that we will not disclose any statement, comment, or disclosure made by any party, expert, consultant, or attorney during the collaborative process to any court for any purpose unless a final settlement agreement is reached or both parties and their attorneys have agreed to the disclosure.

To maintain an objective and constructive process, the parties agree to discuss settlement of divorce issues with each other only in the settlement conference setting. The parties will not discuss these matters with each other outside the conference setting except as mutually agreed by the parties and their attorneys. The parties understand that, from time to time, the attorneys will meet together to plan agendas for settlement meetings, but no agreements will be made by the attorneys on behalf of the parties without their consent.

The parties acknowledge that inappropriate communications regarding settlement of their divorce can be harmful to their minor children. The parties and their attorneys agree that communication with the minor children regarding these issues will occur only as agreed by the parties and their attorneys. In resolving issues about sharing the enjoyment of and responsibility for the children, the parties, attorneys, and therapists will make every effort to reach amicable solutions that promote the children's best interests.

We agree to act quickly to mediate and resolve differences related to the children to promote a caring, loving, and involved relationship between the children and both parents. We agree not to seek a custody evaluation while the matter is a collaborative law case.

The parties agree to insulate the children from involvement in their disputes.

Experts

If experts are needed, we will retain them jointly unless we agree otherwise in writing. We will use neutral experts for purposes of valuation, cash-flow analysis, tax issues, parenting issues, and any other issue that requires expert advice or recommendations. We will agree in advance how each expert will be paid.

The parties agree that any such expert may not be called by either of them as a witness if the parties fail to reach settlement through the collaborative law process.

Either party may use a consultant for assistance in gathering or organizing information as long as all such information gathered or organized by the consultant is made available to the other party as soon as it becomes available.

Information

We agree to deal with each other in good faith and to promptly provide all necessary and reasonable information requested. No formal discovery procedure will be used unless specifically agreed to in advance. The parties will be required to sign a sworn statement making full and fair disclosure of their income, assets, and debts (a sworn inventory and appraisement) unless they agree otherwise in writing.

We acknowledge that, by using informal discovery, we are giving up certain investigative procedures and methods that would be available to us in the litigation process. We give up these measures with the specific understanding that the parties will make to each other a complete and accurate disclosure of all assets, income, debts, and other information necessary for us to reach a fair settlement. Participation in the collaborative law process is based on the assumptions that we have acted in good faith and that the parties have provided complete and accurate information to the best of their ability. The parties and their attorneys further agree to make full disclosure of all material information concerning the parties' children. Refusal to be honest or failure to disclose such information shall be grounds for one or both collaborative attorneys' withdrawal from representation.

Enforceability of Agreements

If we require a temporary agreement for any purpose, the agreement will be put in writing and signed by us. If either party withdraws from the collaborative process, the written agreement may be presented to the court as an agreement enforceable under the laws of this State, which may become a court order and, if required by either party, shall be in the form of an agreed temporary order and entered by the court. A collaborative attorney shall be permitted to present to the court a written agreement that is signed by both parties and the collaborative attorneys for entry of a temporary order.

The parties may agree in writing to the resolution of any or all issues presented by their case. Any written agreement that is signed by both parties and their collaborative attorneys may be filed with the court as a collaborative law settlement agreement in accordance, which the court may make retroactive to the date of the written agreement and which may be made the basis of a court order.

The parties understand and agree that neither collaborative attorney shall be permitted to go to court to enforce any written agreements between the parties. Should a party seek to enforce any written agreement over the objection of the other party, the parties must withdraw from the collaborative law process. In such event, the collaborative attorneys shall withdraw as attorneys of record and, if required, shall consent to the substitution of trial counsel.

Legal Process

The attorneys do not represent both clients. The parties agree that, while the respective attorneys who are also parties to this agreement are committed to negotiation in an atmosphere of honesty and integrity, neither party can look to the attorney representing his or her spouse to provide legal advice or information, and each attorney must continue to have an obligation to represent that attorney's client diligently and cannot be, or represent himself or herself to be, representing the legal interests of the other party.

(Attorney Name) DOES NOT REPRESENT MARY SMITH. (Attorney Name) DOES NOT REPRESENT

JOHN SMITH. NOTHING IN THIS AGREEMENT SHOULD BE INTERPRETED AS OBLIGATING EITHER ATTORNEY TO VIOLATE HIS OR HER ETHICAL OBLIGATIONS TO REPRESENT HIS OR HER CLIENT'S BEST INTERESTS.

Court Proceedings: The parties understand that their attorneys' representation is limited to the collaborative law process and that neither attorney can ever represent one of the parties in court in a proceeding against the other spouse.

If the collaborative law process terminates, both attorneys will be disqualified from representing either client, and consultants will be disqualified as witnesses and the consultants' work product will be inadmissible as evidence unless the parties agree otherwise in writing.

After this date, no motion or document will be prepared or filed without our agreement, other than a petition for divorce, answer and mutual injunctions. Service of citation will not be required. We agree not to seek judicial intervention during the collaborative law process, except for withdrawal or substitution of counsel, unless we agree otherwise.

Withdrawal from Collaborative Law Process: If one of the parties decides to withdraw from the collaborative law process, that party will give prompt written notice to the court, if appropriate, and to the other party through his or her attorney. On withdrawal from the collaborative law process, there will be a thirty-day waiting period (unless there is an emergency) before any court hearing, to permit each party to retain another attorney and make an orderly transition. All temporary agreements will remain in full force and effect during this period. The intent of this provision is to avoid surprise and prejudice to the rights of the other party. Either party may bring this provision to the attention of the court in requesting a postponement of a hearing.

Withdrawal of Counsel: If a party chooses to withdraw from the collaborative process by seeking court involvement, both attorneys shall immediately withdraw from the representation. Further, the parties understand that neither collaborative attorney (or any attorney associated in the practice of law with him or her) may serve as litigation counsel in this case thereafter. Both attorneys will cooperate in transferring the file to new counsel and are authorized to disclose information to prospective future counsel on their respective client's request.

Understandings

The parties understand there is no guarantee that the process will be successful in resolving their case. They understand that the process cannot eliminate concerns about the disharmony, distrust, and irreconcilable differences that have led to their current conflict. They understand that they are still expected to assert their respective interests and that their respective attorneys will help each of them to do so.

The parties further understand that they should not lapse into a false sense of security that the process will protect each of them. They understand that, although their collaborative attorneys share a commitment to the process described in this agreement, each attorney has a professional duty to represent his or her own client diligently and is not the attorney for the other party.

Attorney's Fees and Costs

The parties understand that their attorneys and consultants are entitled to be paid for their services, and the first task in a collaborative matter is to ensure payment to each of them and to make funds available for this purpose. The parties agree to make funds available from their community or separate estates, as needed, to pay these fees. The parties understand that, if necessary, one party may be asked to pay both attorney's fees from community property managed solely by him or her (for example, his or her salary) or from that party's separate property funds. The parties agree that, to the extent possible, all attorney's fees and costs (including expert's fees) incurred by both parties shall be paid in full before entry of an agreed Final Decree/Order.

Participation with Integrity

We will work to protect the privacy, respect, and dignity of all involved, including parties, attorneys, and consultants.

We will maintain a high standard of integrity. Specifically, we will not take advantage of each other or of the miscalculations or mistakes of others; instead, we will identify and correct them.

Acknowledgment

We acknowledge that we have read this agreement, understand its terms and conditions, and agree to abide by them. We understand that by agreeing to this alternative method of resolving the divorce issues, we are giving up certain rights, including the right to conduct formal discovery, the right to participate in formal court hearings, and other rights provided by the adversarial legal system.

_____

                                                   John Smith

_____

                                                   Mary Smith

By: _____

Attorney _____
State Bar No. _____
Attorney for John Smith _____

Signed on _____

By: _____

Attorney _____
State Bar No. _____
Attorney for Mary Smith _____

Signed on _____

Appendix K
Sample Mediated Settlement Agreement

The undersigned parties agree to compromise and settle the claims and controversies between them, including all conservatorship, child support, and possession disputes regarding the above-identified child of the parties and any and all property and debt division disputes. The parties wish to avoid potentially protracted and costly litigation, and agree and stipulate that they have carefully considered the needs of the children, their respective ability and contribution other than in cash, for support, and the best interest of the children. The parties stipulate that the agreements set forth hereinafter are in the children's best interest, and in their own best interest and agree that such issues are resolved. In order to reach this settlement, all claims were considered and resolved. Both parties are satisfied with their attorney's advice but understand this agreement is made by their free will and not forced by the advice or encouragement of their attorneys or the mediator.

The parties agree as follows:

Conservatorship and support
    a. <u>Conservatorship</u>- Parties are named Joint managing conservators with Mother have the right to establish the primary residence of the children within Collin County and the right to receive child support.

    b. <u>Child support and medical support</u>- Father will pay

$_____$ a month in child support with family code step-downs. Father will reimburse Mother the cost of the children's health insurance in the amount of $\$_____$ per month. All uninsured medical expenses are split 50/50 between the parties.

PARTY'S ACCESS WITH THE CHILD SHALL BE AS AGREED TO BY THE PARTIES, IF THE PARTIES CANNOT AGREE THAN AS FOLLOWS:

a. <u>Access-</u> Father will have expanded standard per the for school year, summer and holiday access.

b. <u>Right of First Refusal-</u> The parties agree to a Right of First Refusal if either parent is going to be away from the children overnight.

c. <u>Passport- International Travel-</u> Standard Passport provisions. *Mother will possess the passport and will give to Mother for international trav*el upon request. The parties are allowed to travel with the child internationally so long as the country falls within the Hague Convention.

Injunctions

a. Both parties are enjoined from making disparaging remarks about the other parent around the children or within hearing distance of their child or allow other's to do so or to discuss the fault of the divorce.

b. Both parties are enjoined from having a paramour or significant other they are romantically involved with, reside at their residence unless they are married.

Property Division

a. See attached spreadsheet, Exhibit A attached and incorporated herein. Each party is awarded the asset under their column Wife or Husband or a percentage of the asset as shown if the asset is divided. Parties acknowledge that balances of accounts change daily but all assets are awarded plus gains and losses from today's date.

b. Personal Property- each party is awarded their personal effects, clothing jewellery etc. And Wife is awarded the following currently in Husbands possession: Plaid LR furniture and rug, the ugly wingback chair, elliptical, black refrigerator and small desk. Mother will obtain these items at an agreed upon time within 30 days of this agreement.

c. Federal Taxes- Parties will file Joint taxes for 2015 and each receive 50% of any refund or pay 50% of any money owed on their personal taxes. For 2016 the parties will partition their income.

d. Wife will provide copies of photos in her possession that Husband wants and Husband will provide Wife copies of home videos that she wants.

Miscellaneous

Attorney for Wife will prepare the Final Decree/Order. Both parties acknowledge the orders can be entered based on this Mediated Settlement Agreement.

This mediated settlement agreement is effective as of today, _____.

I understand that this agreement does not preclude other more detailed agreements and decrees. I realize that more detailed documents in the form of an Agreed Decree of Divorce and/ or agreement incident thereto will be drafted by the parties' attorneys.

If there is a disagreement between the parties for the drafting of the final decree, or the interpretation of this agreement, the parties agree to arbitration with _____ to resolve the dispute. These documents, however, are not a condition precedent to the formation of this mediated settlement agreement, but rather are merely a more formal memorial of this already enforceable mediated settlement agreement.

Parties acknowledge they may not have all the of information needed or entitled to prior to resolving this case and they waive that right to obtain that information and are willing to make an agreement regardless of not having all of the documentation to support amounts in various accounts.

THE PARTIES HERETO AGREE THAT THIS AGREEMENT IS BINDING ON THE PARTIES AND IS NOT SUBJECT TO REVOCATION. A PARTY TO THIS AGREEMENT IS ENTITLED TO JUDGMENT ON THIS MEDIATED SETTLEMENT AGREEMENT.

AGREED AND APPROVED on _____ :

_____

Mother/Wife

_____

Father/Husband

_____

Attorney for Mother/
Wife

_____

Attorney for Father/
Husband

Appendix L
Binding Arbritration Sample Agreement

Definition of Arbitration. Arbitration is a process in which an impartial person acts as the decision maker for the case ,if the parties are unable to reach an agreement. The parties acknowledge that they are unable to reach an agreement on to the wording of the final order in the Motions currently on file with the Court. In this particular case the parties agree to have [NAME OF MEDIATOR] arbitrate a final order to be entered with the Court regarding the issues presented at the mediation on [DATE]. The parties agree that the decision made by [NAME OF ARBITRATOR] as arbitrator is binding on the parties as authorized by state law.

Consent to Arbitration. The parties confirm their consent to the [NAME OF ARBITRATOR] as the arbitrator for their case. In addition, the parties agree that the following issues related to their divorce shall be determined by the Arbitrator:

1. How the marital/community property shall be divided including debts and assets.
2. Whether spousal support should be awarded and, if so, how much should be paid and the length of time spousal support, if any, should be paid.
3. All issues regarding the minor children including, but not limited to, custody, possession and access, child support and rights and duties of the parents.
4. Any and all other issues agreed to be arbitrated by the parties.

In addition, the parties agree that the Arbitrator may grant any and all relief the Arbitrator believes is just and right in accordance with the laws governing divorce in this State.

In cases involving custody and/or visitation, the parties may, at the request of the Arbitrator, agree that the Arbitrator may appoint a mental health professional to interview and/or examine the parties and/or their child(ren) and make recommendations to the Arbitrator. If the parties agree to have the Arbitrator make such an appointment, the parties agree:

1. the fees and expenses of the mental health professional so appointed shall be paid by the parties,
2. the mental health professional shall report only to the Arbitrator, and
3. the mental health professional shall be considered as an extension of the Arbitrator and, as such, covered by the Exclusion of Liability provisions of this Agreement which apply to the Arbitrator.

No Record of Session. There shall be no electronic or stenographic record of any session.

Arbitrator's Award. The result of the arbitration will be in the form of an arbitration order scanned and email to the parties. The arbitration order will provide sufficient detail from which the attorneys can draft a Final Decree/Order. The parties agree that the Final Decree drafted by counsel shall be submitted to the Court for adoption and confirmation. The parties understand and agree they will be bound by the Arbitrator's Award and will not seek for any reason for the Arbitrator's Award to be vacated or otherwise set aside except as allowed by State law.

Right to Trial/Appeal. Both parties acknowledge that they have an absolute right to have their divorce litigated in court. They have been advised if this right and freely and voluntarily waive said right. The parties further understand and agree that by participating in binding arbitration they have their right to appeal the Arbitrator's Award except as otherwise provided by State law.

Exclusion of Liability. The arbitrator is not a necessary or proper party in judicial proceedings relating to the arbitration. Neither [NAME OF ARBITRATOR] or any law firm employing [HIM/HER] shall be liable to any party for any act or omission in connection with any mediation conducted under these rules. The Arbitrator shall not be named as a party, called as a witness, be required to show cause, or otherwise appear or respond in any proceeding related to or arising out of his role as arbitrator.

Cost of Arbitrator/Arbitration. The Arbitrator will charge $_____.00/hour, plus any out of pocket expenses. Initially the parties are responsible for the Arbitrator's fees and out of pocket expenses on an equal basis. The arbitrator shall collect deposits (retainers) from the parties in advance for all fees and expenses to be incurred in this matter. The Arbitrator will determine if a different allocation of Arbitrators fee or expenses should be awarded at the conclusion of the arbitration.

AGREED TO on [DATE]:

_____   _____

Mother   Attorney for Mother

_____   _____

Father   Attorney for Father

Appendix M
Inventory and Appraisement (I&A) Sample

Estate of the Parties

1. **Real Property** (include any property purchased by contract for deed, such as property purchased in recreational developments, and time-shares)

    1.1. Street address: _____

    County of location: _____

    Description of improvements, if any: _____

    _____

    Legal description: _____

    _____

    Current fair market value (as of _____):

    $_____

    Name of mortgage company and account number, if any: _____

    Current balance of mortgage (as of _____):

    $_____

    Other liens against property: _____

    _____

    Names of other lienholders: _____

    _____

Current net equity in property: $_____

1.2. Street address: _____

_____

County of location: _____

Description of improvements, if any: _____

_____

Legal description: _____

_____

Current fair market value (as of _____)

$_____

Name of mortgage company and account
number, if any: _____

Current balance of mortgage (as of _____):

$_____

Other liens against property:_____

_____

Names of other lienholders _____

_____

Current net equity in property: $_____

1.3. Street address: _____

_____

County of location: _____

Description of improvements, if any:_____

_____

Legal description: _____

Current fair market value (as of _____):

$_____

Name of mortgage company and account
number, if any:_____

Current balance of mortgage (as of _____):

$_____

Other liens against property:_____

_____

Names of other lienholders:_____

_____

Current net equity in property: $_____

2. **Mineral Interests** (include any property in which the
    parties own the mineral estate, separate and apart from
    the surface estate, such as oil and gas leases; also include
    royalty interests, working interests, and producing and
    nonproducing oil and gas wells)

    2.1. Name of mineral interest/lease/well: _____

          Type of interest: _____

          County of location: _____

          Legal description: _____

          Name of producer/operator: _____

          Current value (as of _____):

          $_____

    2.2   Name of mineral interest/lease/well: _____

Type of interest: _____

County of location: _____

Legal description: _____

Name of producer/operator: _____

Current value (as of _____):

$_____

2.3. Name of mineral interest/lease/well: _____

Type of interest: _____

County of location: _____

Legal description: _____

Name of producer/operator: _____

Current value (as of _____):

$_____

3. **Cash and Accounts with Financial Institutions** (include cash, traveler's checks, money orders, and accounts with commercial banks, savings banks, credit unions, and funds on deposit with attorneys and other third parties; exclude accounts with brokerage houses and all retirement accounts)

3.1. Cash on hand: $_____

3.2. Traveler's checks: $_____

3.3. Money orders: $_____

3.4. Name of financial institution: _____

Account name: _____

Account number: _____

Type of account: (checking/savings/money
market/certificate of deposit) _____

_____

Name(s) on withdrawal cards: _____

_____

Current account balance (as of _____):

$_____

3.5. Name of financial institution: _____

Account name: _____

Account number: _____

Type of account: (checking/savings/money
market/certificate of deposit) _____

_____

Name(s) on withdrawal cards: _____

_____

Current account balance (as of _____):

$_____

3.6. Name of financial institution: _____

Account name: _____

Account number: _____

Type of account: (checking/savings/money
market/certificate of deposit) _____

_____

Name(s) on withdrawal cards: _____

_____

Current account balance (as of _____):

$_____

3.7.   Name of financial institution: _____

Account name: _____

Account number: _____

Type of account: (checking/savings/money
market/certificate of deposit) _____

_____

Name(s) on withdrawal cards: _____

_____

Current account balance (as of _____):

$_____

4.   Brokerage and Mutual Fund Accounts

4.1.   Name of brokerage firm or mutual fund:

_____

Address of brokerage firm or mutual fund:

_____

_____

Name account held in: _____

Name of account (and subaccounts if any):

_____

Account number (and numbers of subaccounts if any): _____

_____

Margin loan balance (as of _____):

$_____

Value of community interest in each account (and subaccounts if any) (as of _____):

$_____

Tax basis of each security held: $_____

4.2. Name of brokerage firm or mutual fund:

_____

Address of brokerage firm or mutual fund:

_____

_____

Name account held in: _____

Name of account (and subaccounts if any):

_____

Account number (and numbers of subaccounts if any): _____

_____

Margin loan balance (as of _____):

$_____

Value of community/marital interest in each account (and subaccounts if any) (as of _____):

$_____

Tax basis of each security held: $_____

4.3.   Name of brokerage firm or mutual fund:

_____

Address of brokerage firm or mutual fund:

_____

_____

Name account held in: _____

Name of account (and subaccounts if any):

_____

Account number (and numbers of subaccounts
if any): _____

_____

Margin loan balance (as of _____):

$_____

Value of community/marital interest in each
account (and subaccounts if any) (as of _____):

$_____

Tax basis of each security held: $_____

5.   **Publicly Traded Stocks, Bonds, and Other Securities**
(include securities not in a brokerage account, mutual
fund, or retirement fund)

5.1.   Name of security: _____

Number of shares: _____

Type of security: [common stock/preferred
stock/bond/other security]: _____

Certificate numbers: _____

In possession of: _____

Name of exchange on which listed: _____

Pledged as collateral? [Yes/No]

Date acquired: _____

Tax basis: $_____

Current market value (as of _____):

$_____

Value of community/marital interest (as of ____):

$_____

5.2. Name of security: _____

Number of shares: _____

Type of security: [common stock/preferred stock/bond/other security]: _____

Certificate numbers: _____

In possession of: _____

Name of exchange on which listed: _____

Pledged as collateral? [Yes/No]

Date acquired: _____

Tax basis: $_____

Current market value (as of _____):

$_____

Value of community/marital interest (as of ____):

$_____

6. **Stock Options** (include all exercisable, non-exercisable, vested and non-vested stock options regardless of any restrictions on transfer)

6.1. Name of company: _____

Date of option/grant: _____

Vesting schedule: _____

Number of options: _____

Are the options exercisable? [Yes/No]

Are the options registered? [Yes/No]

Current stock price: $_____

Strike price: $_____

If purchased, total purchase price of option contract (including commissions):

$_____

Current net market value (as of _____):

$_____

Value of community interest (as of _____):

$_____

6.2. Name of company: _____

Date of option/grant: _____

Vesting schedule: _____

Number of options: _____

Are the options exercisable? [Yes/No]

Are the options registered? [Yes/No]

Current stock price: $_____

Strike price: $_____

If purchased, total purchase price of option contract (including commissions):

$_____

Current net market value (as of _____):

$_____

Value of community interest (as of _____):

$_____

7. **Bonuses**

   7.1. Name of company: _____

   Spouse earning bonus: _____

   Date bonus expected to be paid: _____

   Time period covered by bonus: _____

   Anticipated amount of bonus: $_____

   7.2. Name of company: _____

   Spouse earning bonus: _____

   Date bonus expected to be paid: _____

   Time period covered by bonus: _____

   Anticipated amount of bonus: $_____

8. **Closely Held Business Interests** (include sole proprietorships, professional practices, corporations, partnerships, limited liability companies and partnerships, joint ventures, and other non-publicly traded business entities)

8.1. Name of business: _____

Address: _____

Type of business organization: _____

Percentage of ownership: _____

Number of shares owned (if applicable): _____

Value (as of _____):

$_____

Balance of accounts receivable if on cash basis accounting:

$_____

Balance of liabilities if on cash basis accounting:

<$_____>

9. **Retirement Benefits**

9.A. *Defined Contribution Plans* (a plan that provides for an individual account for a participant and for benefits based solely on the amount contributed to the participant's account; IRC §§ 401(k), 403(b))

9.A.1. Exact name of plan: _____

Name and address of plan administrator:

_____

Employee: _____

Employer: _____

Starting date of creditable service: _____

Account name: _____

Account number: _____

Account balance as of date of marriage: $_____

Payee of survivor benefits: _____

Designated beneficiary: _____

Current account balance (as of _____): $_____

Balance of loan against plan: $_____

Value of community interest in plan (as of _____): $_____

9.A.2. Exact name of plan: _____

Name and address of plan administrator:

_____

Employee: _____

Employer: _____

Starting date of creditable service: _____

Account name: _____

Account number: _____

Account balance as of date of marriage: $_____

Payee of survivor benefits: _____

Designated beneficiary: _____

Current account balance (as of _____): $_____

Balance of loan against plan: $_____

Value of community interest in plan (as of _____):

$_____

9.B.   *Defined Benefit Plan* (any plan that is not a defined contribution plan and that usually involves payment of benefits according to a formula)

9.B.1.   Exact name of plan: _____

Name and address of plan administrator:

_____

Employee: _____

Employer: _____

Starting date of creditable service: _____

Designated beneficiary: _____

Payee of survivor benefits: _____

Description of benefits: _____

_____

Value of community interest in plan (as of _____):

$_____

9.B.2.   Exact name of plan: _____

Name and address of plan administrator:

_____

Employee: _____

Employer: _____

Starting date of creditable service: _____

Designated beneficiary: _____

Payee of survivor benefits: _____

Description of benefits: _____

_____

Value of community interest in plan (as of _____):

$_____

9.C. *IRA/SEP*

9.C.1. Name of financial institution: _____

Account name: _____

Account number: _____

Payee of survivor benefits: _____

Designated beneficiary: _____

Current account balance (as of _____):

$_____

Value of community interest (as of _____):

$_____

9.C.2. Name of financial institution: _____

Account name: _____

Account number: _____

Payee of survivor benefits: _____

Designated beneficiary: _____

Current account balance (as of _____):

$_____

Value of community interest (as of

_____):

$_____

9.D. *Military Benefits*

9.D.1. Branch of service: _____

Name of service member: _____

Rank/pay grade of service member: ____

_____

Starting date of creditable service:

_____

Status of service member: [active/
reserve/retired] _____

Payee of survivor benefits: _____

Description of benefits: _____

Monthly benefit payable: $_____

Value of community/martial interest in
plan (as of _____):

$_____

Percentage of plan that is community/
martial property: _____%

9.D.2. Branch of service: _____

Name of service member: _____

Rank/pay grade of service member: _____

Starting date of creditable service:

Status of service member: [active/ reserve/retired] _____

Payee of survivor benefits: _____

Description of benefits: _____

Monthly benefit payable: $_____

Value of community/martial interest in plan (as of _____):

$_____

Percentage of plan that is community/ martial property: _____%

9.E. *Nonqualified Plans (Not under ERISA)*

  9.E.1. Name of financial institution: _____

   Account name: _____

   Account number: _____

   Account balance as of date of marriage:

   $_____

   Payee of survivor benefits: _____

   Designated beneficiary: _____

   Value of community interest in plan (as of _____):

   $_____

9.E.2. Name of financial institution: _____

_____

Account name: _____

Account number: _____

Account balance as of date of marriage:

$_____

Payee of survivor benefits: _____

Designated beneficiary: _____

Value of community interest in plan (as
of _____):

$_____

9.F. *Government Benefits (civil service, teacher,
railroad, state and local)*

9.F.1. Name of plan: _____

Account name: _____

Account number: _____

Account balance as of date of marriage:

$_____

Payee of survivor benefits: _____

Designated beneficiary: _____

_____

Value of community interest in plan (as
of _____):

$_____

9.F.2. Name of plan: _____

Account name: _____

Account number: _____

Account balance as of date of marriage:
$_____

Payee of survivor benefits: _____

Designated beneficiary: _____

_____

Value of community interest in plan (as
of _____):

$_____

10. **Other Deferred Compensation Benefits** (e.g., worker's compensation, disability benefits, other "special payments", and other forms of compensation)

10.1. Husband

Description of Asset	Value

10.2 Wife

Description of Asset	Value

11. **Union Benefits** (include all insurance, pensions, retirement benefits, and other benefits arising out of membership in any union)

   11.1. Name of union member: _____

       Name of Union: _____

       Description of benefits: _____

       Value (as of _____):

       $_____

   11.2. Name of union member: _____

       Name of Union: _____

       Description of benefits: _____

       Value (as of _____):

       $_____

12. **Insurance and Annuities**

   12.A. *Life Insurance*

       12.A.1. Name of insurance company: _____

           _____

           Policy number: _____

           Name of insured: _____

           Name of owner: _____

           Type of insurance: [term/whole/universal] _____

           Amount of premiums:

$_____

Date of issue: _____

Face amount: _____

Cash surrender value on date of
marriage:

$_____

Current cash surrender value: _____

Designated beneficiary: _____

Balance of loan against policy: $_____

Value of community/martial interest

(as of _____):

$_____

12.A.2. Name of insurance company: _____

_____

Policy number: _____

Name of insured: _____

Name of owner: _____

Type of insurance: [term/whole/univer-
sal] _____

Amount of premiums:

$_____

Date of issue: _____

Face amount: _____

Cash surrender value on date of
marriage:

$_____

Current cash surrender value: _____

Designated beneficiary: _____

Balance of loan against policy: $_____

Value of community/martial interest

(as of _____):

$_____

12.B. *Annuities*

12.B.1. Name of company: _____

Policy number: _____

Name of annuitant: _____

Name of owner: _____

Type of annuity: _____

Amount of premiums: $_____

Date of issue: _____

Face amount: _____

Designated beneficiary: _____

Value on date of marriage: _____

Current value (as of _____):

$_____

Balance of loan against policy: $_____

Value of community/marital interest

(as of _____):

$_____

12.B.2. Name of company: _____

Policy number: _____

Name of annuitant: _____

Name of owner: _____

Type of annuity: _____

Amount of premiums: $_____

Date of issue: _____

Face amount: _____

Designated beneficiary: _____

Value on date of marriage: _____

Current value (as of _____):

$_____

Balance of loan against policy: $_____

Value of community/marital interest

(as of _____):

$_____

12.C. *Health Savings Accounts*

12.C.1.Institution holding account: _____

_____

Account number: _____

Name of high-deductible health plan
with which the HSA is coupled: _____

_____

Value of assets in account (as of _____):

$_____

12.C.2. Institution holding account: _____

_____

Account number: _____

Name of high-deductible health plan
with which the HSA is coupled: _____

_____

Value of assets in account (as of _____):
$_____

12.D. *Medical Savings Accounts*

12.D.1. Institution holding account: _____

_____

Account number: _____

Name of high-deductible health plan
with which the MSA is coupled: _____

_____

Value of assets in account (as of _____):
$_____

12.D.2. Institution holding account: _____

_____

Account number: _____

Name of high-deductible health plan
with which the MSA is coupled: _____

_____

Value of assets in account (as of _____):
$_____

13. **Motor Vehicles, Boats, Airplanes, Cycles, etc.** (including mobile homes, trailers, and recreational vehicles; exclude company-owned vehicles)

13.1. Year: _____

    Make: _____

    Model: _____

    Name on title: _____

    In possession of: _____

    Vehicle identification number: _____

    Name of creditor if loan against vehicle: _____

    _____

    Current balance (as of _____):

    $_____

    Current fair market value of vehicle (as of _____):

    $_____

    Current net equity in vehicle: $_____

13.2. Year: _____

    Make: _____

    Model: _____

    Name on title: _____

    In possession of: _____

    Vehicle identification number: _____

    Name of creditor if loan against vehicle: _____

    _____

    Current balance (as of _____):

$_____

Current fair market value of vehicle (as of ____):

$_____

Current net equity in vehicle: $_____

14. **Money Owed to Me or My Spouse** (include any expected federal or state income tax refund but do not include receivables connected with a business)

14.1. Name of debtor: _____

Debtor's relationship to you: _____

Is debt evidenced in writing? [Yes/No]

Is debt secured? [Yes/No]

Current loan amount owed (as of _____):

$_____

14.2. Name of debtor: _____

Debtor's relationship to you: _____

Is debt evidenced in writing? [Yes/No]

Is debt secured? [Yes/No]

Current loan amount owed (as of _____):

$_____

15. **Household Furniture, Furnishings, and Fixtures**

15.1. In possession of husband (attach separate sheet by room if necessary):

Description of Asset	Value

15.2. In possession of wife (attach separate sheet by room if necessary):

Description of Asset	Value

16. Electronics and Computers

16.1. In possession of husband (attach separate sheet if necessary):

Description of Asset	Value

16.2. In possession of wife (attach separate sheet if necessary):

Description of Asset	Value

17. **Antiques, Artwork, and Collections** (include any works of art, such as paintings, tapestry, rugs, and coin or stamp collections)

    17.1. In possession of husband (attach separate sheet if necessary):

Description of Asset	Value

    17.2. In possession of wife (attach separate sheet if necessary):

Description of Asset	Value

18. **Miscellaneous Sporting Goods and Firearms**

    18.1. In possession of husband (attach separate sheet if necessary):

Description of Asset	Value

    18.2. In possession of wife (attach separate sheet if necessary):

Description of Asset	Value

19. **Jewelry and Other Personal Items**

    19.1. In possession of husband (attach separate sheet if necessary):

Description of Asset	Value

19.2. In possession of wife (attach separate sheet if necessary):

Description of Asset	Value

20. Livestock (include cattle, horses, and so forth)

20.1. In possession of husband (attach separate sheet if necessary):

Description of Asset	Value

20.2. In possession of wife (attach separate sheet if necessary):

Description of Asset	Value

21. **Club Memberships**

    21.1. Name of club: _____

        Name membership held in: _____

        Account number: _____

        Current value (as of _____):

        $_____

        Method of valuation: _____

22. **Travel Award Benefits** (include frequent-flyer mileage accounts)

    22.1. Name of airline: _____

        Account number and name on account: _____

        _____

        Current number of miles (as of _____):

        _____

        Current value (if any): $_____

23. **Miscellaneous Assets** (include intellectual property, licenses, crops, farm equipment, construction equipment, tools, leases, cemetery lots, gold or silver coins not part of a collection described elsewhere in this inventory, estimated tax payments, tax overpayments, loss carry-forward deductions, lottery tickets/winnings, stadium bonds, stadium seat licenses, seat options, and season tickets)

    23.1. In possession of husband (attach separate sheet if necessary):

Description of Asset	Value

23.2. In possession of wife (attach separate sheet if necessary):

Description of Asset	Value

24. Safe-Deposit Boxes

24.1. Name of financial institution or other depository: _____

Box number: _____

Names of persons with access to contents: _____

_____

Items in safe-deposit box: _____

_____

25. Storage Facilities

25.1. Name and location: _____

Unit number: _____

Terms and length of lease: _____

_____

Names of persons with access to contents: _____

_____

Items in storage unit: _____

_____

26. Community/Marital Claim for Reimbursement

26.1. Reimbursement claim against husband's separate estate: _____

Basis of claim: _____

Amount claimed (as of _____):

$_____

26.2. Reimbursement claim against wife's separate estate: _____

Basis of claim: _____

Amount claimed (as of _____):

$_____

27. Contingent Assets (e.g., lawsuits by either party against third party)

27.1. Nature of claim: _____

Amount of claim: $_____

27.2. Nature of claim: _____

Amount of claim: $_____

28. **Community/Martial Liabilities**

28.A. *Credit Cards and Charge Accounts*

28.A.1. Name of creditor: _____

Account number: _____

Name(s) on account: _____

Current balance (as of _____):

<$_____>

Balance as of _____ [date of separation]:

<$_____>

28.A.2. Name of creditor: _____

Account number: _____

Name(s) on account: _____

Current balance (as of _____):

<$_____>

Balance as of _____ [date of separation]:

<$_____>

28.A.3. Name of creditor: _____

Account number: _____

Name(s) on account: _____

Current balance (as of _____):

<$_____>

Balance as of _____ [date of separation]:

<$_____>

28.A.4. Name of creditor: _____

Account number: _____

Name(s) on account: _____

Current balance (as of _____):

<$_____>

Balance as of _____ [date of separation]:

<$_____>

28.A.5. Name of creditor: _____

Account number: _____

Name(s) on account: _____

Current balance (as of _____):

<$_____>

Balance as of _____ [date of separation]:

<$_____>

28.B. *Federal, State, and Local Tax Liability*

28.B.1. Amount owed in any previous tax year:

<$_____>

[describe liability, e.g., federal income tax/property taxes]:

_____

_____

Amount owed for current year:

<$_____>

28.B.2. Amount owed in any previous tax year:

<$_____>

[describe liability, e.g., federal income tax/property taxes]:

_____

_____

Amount owed for current year:

<$_____>

28.C. *Attorney's Fees in This Case*

28.C.1. Husband (as of _____):

<$_____>

28.C.2. Wife (as of _____):

<$_____>

28.D. *Other Professional Fees in This Case*

28.D.1.   Husband (as of _____):

<$_____>

28.D.2.   Wife (as of _____):

<$_____>

28.E. *Other Liabilities Not Otherwise Listed in This Inventory* (e.g., loans, margin accounts, if not previously disclosed)

28.E.1. Name of creditor: _____

Account number: _____

Party incurring liability: _____

Is loan evidenced in writing? [Yes/No]

Current balance (as of _____):

<$_____>

Security, if any: _____

28.E.2. Name of creditor: _____

Account number: _____

Party incurring liability: _____

Is loan evidenced in writing? [Yes/No]

Current balance (as of _____):

<$_____>

Security, if any: _____

28.E.3. Name of creditor: _____

Account number: _____

Party incurring liability: _____

Is loan evidenced in writing? [Yes/No]

Current balance (as of _____):

<$_____>

Security, if any: _____

28.F. *Reimbursement Claims against Communit/
Marital Estate*

28.F.1. Reimbursement claim by husband's
separate estate: _____

Basis of claim: _____

_____

Amount claimed (as of _____):

$_____

28.F.2. Reimbursement claim by wife's separate
estate: _____

Basis of claim: _____

_____

Amount claimed (as of _____):

$_____

28.G. *Pledges* (include charitable, church and school
related)

28.G.1.Name and address of recipient: _____

_____

Date of pledge: _____

Total amount of pledge: <_____>

Is pledge payable in installments? [Yes/
No]

Date each installment payment is due:

_____

Amount of each installment: _____

28.H. *Contingent Liabilities* (e.g., lawsuit against either party, guaranty either party may have signed)

28.H.1. Name of creditor: _____

Name of person primarily liable: _____

_____

Amount of contingent liability: <$____>

Nature of contingency: _____

28.H.2. Name of creditor: _____

Name of person primarily liable: _____

_____

Amount of contingent liability: <$____>

Nature of contingency: _____

Separate Estates of the Parties

29. **Separate Assets of Husband** (generally defined as assets owned before marriage or assets acquired during marriage by gift or inheritance or as a result of personal injury)

29.1. Description of asset: _____

Date property acquired: _____

How acquired (e.g., by gift, by devise, by descent, or owned before marriage): _____

_____

Value (as of _____): $_____

29.2. Husband's separate reimbursement claim against community/marital estate: _____

Basis of claim: _____

Amount claimed (as of _____):

$_____

29.3. Husband's separate reimbursement claim against wife's separate estate: _____

Basis of claim: _____

Value (as of _____):

$_____

30. **Liabilities of Husband's Separate Estate**

30.1. Description of liability: _____

Date of liability: _____

How liability acquired: _____

Amount of liability (as of _____):

<$_____>

30.2. Wife's separate reimbursement claim against husband's separate estate: _____

Basis of claim: _____

Value (as of _____):

$_____

30.3. Community estate's reimbursement claim
against husband's separate estate: _____

Basis of claim: _____

Value (as of _____):

$_____

31. **Separate Assets of Wife** (generally defined as assets
owned before marriage or assets acquired during marriage by gift or inheritance or as a result of personal
injury)

31.1. Description of asset: _____

Date property acquired: _____

How acquired (e.g., by gift, by devise, by
descent, or owned before marriage): _____

_____

Value (as of _____):

$_____

31.2. Wife's separate reimbursement claim against
community estate: _____

Basis of claim: _____

Value (as of _____):

$_____

31.3. Wife's separate reimbursement claim against husband's separate estate: _____

Basis of claim: _____

Value (as of _____):

$_____

32. Liabilities of Wife's Separate Estate

32.1. Description of liability: _____

Date of liability: _____

How liability acquired: _____

Amount of liability (as of _____):

<$_____>

32.2. Husband's separate property reimbursement claim against wife's separate estate: _____

_____

Basis of claim: _____

Amount claimed (as of _____):

$_____

32.3. Community estate's reimbursement claim against wife's separate estate: _____

_____

Basis of claim: _____

Amount claimed (as of _____):

$_____

Child's Property

33. **Child's Property**

A. *Custodial Account under Uniform Transfers to Minors Act*

33.A.1. Name of financial institution: _____

_____

Address of financial institution: _____

_____

Name of account: _____

Account number: _____

Amount on deposit (as of _____):

$_____

Name of minor for whom funds were deposited: _____

33.A.2. Name of financial institution: _____

_____

Address of financial institution: _____

_____

Name of account: _____

Account number: _____

Amount on deposit (as of _____):

$_____

Name of minor for whom funds were
deposited: _____

B.   *529 Plan*

33.B.1. Institution or entity administering plan:

_____

Designated beneficiary: _____
Type of plan: _____
Value of assets in plan (as of _____):
$_____

33.B.2. Institution or entity administering plan:

_____

Designated beneficiary: _____
Type of plan: _____
Value of assets in plan (as of _____):
$_____

Trust and Estate Assets

34. **Assets Held by Either Party for the Benefit of Another**
(include formal and informal trusts)

34.1. Name(s) of person(s) holding assets: _____

_____

Description of assets: _____

_____

_____

Name and title of fiduciary (e.g., executor, trustee): _____

_____

Name of owner of beneficial interest: _____

Value of assets (as of _____):

$_____

34.2. Name(s) of person(s) holding assets: _____

_____

Description of assets: _____

_____

Name and title of fiduciary (e.g., executor, trustee): _____

_____

Name of owner of beneficial interest: _____

Value of assets (as of _____):

$_____

35. **Assets Held for the Benefit of Either Party as a Beneficiary** (include formal and informal trusts)

35.1. Name(s) of person(s) holding assets: _____

_____

Description of assets: _____

_____

Name and title of fiduciary (e.g., executor, trustee): _____

_____

Name of owner of beneficial interest: _____

Value of assets (as of _____):

$_____

Verification

I, _____, state on oath that, to the best of my knowledge and belief, this inventory and appraisement contains -

1. a full and complete list of all properties that I claim belong to the community estate of me and my spouse, with the values thereof;

2. a full and complete list of all properties in my possession or subject to my control that I claim or admit are my or my spouse's separate property and estate, with the values thereof; and

3. a full and complete list of the debts that I claim are community indebtedness.

Any omission from this inventory is not intentional but is done through mere inadvertence and not to mislead my spouse. There may be other assets and liabilities of which my spouse is aware, and the omission of those items from this inventory should not be construed as a waiver of my interest in them.

SIGNED BY _____

SIGNED under oath before me on _____.

Notary Public, State of _____

Appendix N
2/2/3 Possession Schedule Sample Language

IT IS ORDERED that each conservator shall comply with all terms and conditions of this Possession Order. IT IS ORDERED that this Possession Order is effective _____ and applies to all periods of possession occurring on and after the date the Court signs this Possession Order. IT IS, THEREFORE, ORDERED:

(a) Definitions
  1. In this Possession Order, "school" means the primary or secondary school in which the child is enrolled or, if the child is not enrolled in a primary or secondary school, the public school district in which the child primarily resides.
  2. In this Possession Order, "child" includes each child, whether one or more, who is a subject of this suit while that child is under the age of eighteen years and not otherwise emancipated.

(b) Mutual Agreement or Specified Terms for Possession

IT IS ORDERED that the conservators shall have possession of the child at times mutually agreed to in advance by the parties, and, in the absence of mutual agreement, it is ORDERED that the conservators shall have possession of the child under the specified terms set out in this Possession Order.

(c) Weekend and Weekday Possession

MOTHER shall have the right to possession of the child as follows:

1. Monday and Tuesday—On Monday and Tuesday every week beginning at 8:00 a.m. on Monday morning and ending at the time the child's school resumes on Wednesday morning or 8:00 a.m. when school is not in session.

2. Weekends—Every other Friday, Saturday, and Sunday, beginning at the time school resumes on Friday morning and ending at the time the child's school resumes on Monday morning. Beginning Friday, January 19, 2007 and every other weekend thereafter. If school is not in session, beginning at 8:00 a.m. on Friday and ending at 8:00 a.m. the following Monday.

FATHER shall have the right to possession of the child as follows:

1. Wednesday and Thursday—On Wednesday and Thursday of each week beginning at the time school resumes on Wednesday morning or at 8:00 a.m. when school is not in session and ending at the time school resumes on Friday morning or 8:00 a.m. when school is not in session.

2. Weekends—Every other Friday, Saturday, and Sunday, beginning at the time school resumes on Friday morning and ending at the time the child's school resumes on Monday morning. Beginning Friday, January 26, 2007 and every other weekend thereafter. If school is not in session, beginning at 8:00

a.m. on Friday and ending at 8:00 a.m. the following Monday.

IT IS ORDERED that in calculating the weekend
periods of possession, the periods shall continue to count for
the purposes of alternating them even if they are superseded
by Spring Break, Extended Summer, or Holiday periods of
possession. This possession schedule shall continue during
the summer months save and except for the provisions below
regarding extended summer possession by each parent:

(d) Spring Break and Extended Summer Possession for
MOTHER

Notwithstanding the weekend and weekday (non-holiday) periods of possession ORDERED for FATHER, it is
explicitly ORDERED that MOTHER shall have a superior
right of possession of the child as follows:

1. Spring Break in Even-Numbered Years–In even-
   numbered years, beginning at the time the child's
   school is regularly dismissed on the day the child is
   dismissed from school for the school's spring vacation and ending at the time school resumes after
   that vacation.

2. Extended Summer Possession by MOTHER—

First Choice in Odd-Numbered Years With Written Notice
by April 1st. If MOTHER gives FATHER written notice
by April 1st of an odd-numbered year specifying an extended
period of summer possession for that year, MOTHER shall
have possession of the child for fourteen consecutive days specified in the written notice beginning no earlier than the day

after the child's school is dismissed for the summer vacation and ending no later than seven days before school resumes at the end of the summer vacation in that year. These periods of possession shall begin and end at 6:00 p.m.

Without Written Notice by April 1 in Odd-Numbered Years—If MOTHER does not give FATHER written notice by April 1 of an odd-numbered year specifying an extended period of summer possession for that year, MOTHER shall have possession of the child beginning Sunday of the first full week of July for fourteen days beginning at 6:00 p.m. and ending at 6:00 p.m. on Sunday.

Second Choice in Even-Numbered Years With Written Notice by April 15th—If MOTHER gives FATHER written notice by April 15 of an even-numbered year specifying an extended period of summer possession for that year, MOTHER shall have possession of the child for fourteen days as specified in the written notice beginning no earlier than the day after the child's school is dismissed for the summer vacation and ending no later than seven days before school resumes at the end of the summer vacation in that year, provided that the period or periods of extended summer possession do not interfere with FATHER's period of Extended Summer Possession in that year. These periods of possession shall begin and end at 6:00 p.m.

Without Written Notice by April 15 in Even-Numbered Years–If MOTHER does not give FATHER written notice by April 15 of an even-numbered year specifying an extended period or periods of summer possession for that year, MOTHER shall have possession of the child for fourteen days beginning at 6:00 p.m. on the Sunday of the third full week of July and ending fourteen days later at 6:00 P.M.

(e) Spring Break and Extended Summer Possession for FATHER

Notwithstanding the weekend and weekday (non-holiday) periods of possession ORDERED for MOTHER, it is explicitly ORDERED that FATHER shall have a superior right of possession of the child as follows:

1. Spring Break in Odd-Numbered Years–In odd-numbered years, beginning at the time the child's school is regularly dismissed on the day the child is dismissed from school for the school's spring vacation and ending at the time school resumes after that vacation.

2. Extended Summer Possession by FATHER—

First Choice in Even-Numbered Years With Written Notice by April 1st. If FATHER gives MOTHER written notice by April 1st of an even-numbered year specifying an extended period of summer possession for that year, FATHER shall have possession of the child for fourteen consecutive days specified in the written notice beginning no earlier than the day after the child's school is dismissed for the summer vacation and ending no later than seven days before school resumes at the end of the summer vacation in that year. These periods of possession shall begin and end at 6:00 p.m.

Without Written Notice by April 1 in Even-Numbered Years–If FATHER does not give MOTHER written notice by April 1 of an Even-Numbered year specifying an extended period of summer possession for that year, FATHER shall have possession of the child beginning the Sunday of the first full week of July for fourteen days beginning at 6:00 p.m. and ending at 6:00 p.m. on Sunday.

Second Choice in Odd-Numbered Years With Written Notice by April 15th.—If FATHER gives MOTHER written notice by April 15 of an odd-numbered year specifying an extended period of summer possession for that year, FATHER shall have possession of the child for fourteen days as specified in the written notice beginning no earlier than the day after the child's school is dismissed for the summer vacation and ending no later than seven days before school resumes at the end of the summer vacation in that year, provided that the period or periods of extended summer possession do not interfere with MOTHER's period of Extended Summer Possession in that year. These periods of possession shall begin and end at 6:00 p.m.

Without Written Notice by April 15 in Odd-Numbered Years–If FATHER does not give MOTHER written notice by April 15 of an even-numbered year specifying an extended period or periods of summer possession for that year, FATHER shall have possession of the child for fourteen days beginning at 6:00 p.m. on the Sunday of the third full week of July and ending fourteen days later at 6:00 P.M. on Sunday.

(f) Holiday Possession

Notwithstanding the weekend, weekday, Spring Break, and Extended Summer periods of possession of the parties, MOTHER and FATHER shall have the right to possession of the child as follows:

1. Christmas Holidays in Even-Numbered Years–In even-numbered years, MOTHER shall have the right to possession of the child beginning at the time the child's school is regularly dismissed on

the day the child is dismissed from school for the Christmas school vacation and ending at noon on December 26, and FATHER shall have the right to possession of the child beginning at noon on December 26 and ending at the time school resumes after that Christmas school vacation.

2. Christmas Holidays in Odd-numbered Years—In odd-numbered years, FATHER shall have the right to possession of the child beginning at the time the child's school is regularly dismissed on the day the child is dismissed from school for the Christmas school vacation and ending at noon on December 26, and MOTHER shall have the right to possession of the child beginning at noon on December 26 and ending at the time the child's school resumes after that Christmas school vacation.

3. Thanksgiving in Odd-numbered Years—In odd-numbered years, MOTHER shall have the right to possession of the child beginning at the time the child's school is regularly dismissed on the day the child is dismissed from school for the Thanksgiving holiday and ending at the time the child's school resumes after that Thanksgiving holiday.

4. Thanksgiving in Even-Numbered Years—In even-numbered years, FATHER shall have the right to possession of the child beginning at the time the child's school is regularly dismissed on the day the child is dismissed from school for the Thanksgiving holiday and ending at the time the child's school resumes after that Thanksgiving holiday.

5. Child's Birthday—If a conservator is not otherwise entitled under this Possession Order to present pos-

session of the child on the child's birthday, that conservator shall have possession of the child beginning at 6:00 p.m. and ending at 8:00 p.m. on that day, provided that conservator picks up the child from the other conservator's residence and returns the child to that same place.

6. Father's Day—FATHER shall have the right to possession of the child each year, beginning at 8:00 a.m. on the Friday preceding Father's Day and ending at 8:00 p.m. on Father's Day, provided that if FATHER is not otherwise entitled under this Possession Order to present possession of the child, he shall pick up the child from the other conservator's residence and return the child to that same place.

Mother's Day—MOTHER shall have the right to possession of the child each year, beginning at 8:00 a.m. on the Friday preceding Mother's Day and ending at 8:00 p.m. on Mother's Day, provided that if MOTHER is not otherwise entitled under this Possession Order to present possession of the child, she shall pick up the child from the other conservator's residence and return the child to that same place.

(f) General Terms and Conditions

Except as otherwise explicitly provided in this Possession Order, the terms and conditions of possession of the child are as follows:

1. Surrender of Child by MOTHER—MOTHER is ORDERED to surrender the child to FATHER at the beginning of each period of FATHER's possession at the MOTHER's residence. If a period

of possession by FATHER begins at the time the child's school resumes or is dismissed, MOTHER is ORDERED to surrender the child to FATHER at the beginning of each such period of possession at the school in which the child is enrolled.

If the child is not in school, FATHER shall pick up the child at the MOTHER's residence at 8:00 a.m., and MOTHER is ORDERED to surrender the child to FATHER at the MOTHER's residence at 8:00 a.m. under these circumstances.

2. Surrender of Child by FATHER–FATHER is ORDERED to surrender the child to MOTHER at the beginning of each period of MOTHER's possession at the FATHER's residence.

If a period of possession by MOTHER begins at the time the child's school resumes or is regularly dismissed, FATHER is ORDERED to surrender the child to MOTHER at the beginning of each such period of possession at the school in which the child is enrolled.

If the child is not in school, MOTHER shall pick up the child at the FATHER's residence at 8:00 a.m., and FATHER is ORDERED to surrender the child to MOTHER at the FATHER's residence at 8:00 a.m. under these circumstances.

3. Personal Effects–Each Conservator is ORDERED to ensure that the child has an adequate supply of clothes and school uniforms at their own residence. Each Conservator is ORDERED to return with the child the personal effects that the child brought at the beginning of the period of possession that belong at the other parent's residence.

4. Designation of Competent Adult–Each conservator may designate any competent adult to pick up and return the child, as applicable. IT IS ORDERED that a conservator or a designated competent adult be present when the child is picked up or returned.

5. Inability to Exercise Possession–Each conservator is ORDERED to give as much advance notice as possible to the person in possession of the child on each occasion that the conservator will be unable to exercise that conservator's right of possession for any specified period.

6. Written Notice–Written notice shall be deemed to have been timely made if received or postmarked before or at the time that notice is due.

7. Telephone Access—Each parent shall be allowed reasonable telephone access with the child when the child is in the other parent's possession. Reasonable is considered one telephone call per day for a duration not to exceed approximately ten minutes.

8. Child Care Costs—Each parent shall be responsible for any child care costs incurred while the child is in that parent's possession, including but not limited to after school care, summer care, and camps.

Duration

The periods of possession ordered above apply to the child the subject of this suit while that child is under the age of eighteen years and not otherwise emancipated.

Appendix O
Alternating Weeks (Week On / Week Off) Sample Language

Possession and Access

(a) Definitions
  1. In this Possession Order "school" means the primary or secondary school in which the child is enrolled or, if the child is not enrolled in a primary or secondary school, the public school district in which the child primarily resides.
  2. In this Possession Order "child" includes each child, whether one or more, who is a subject of this suit while that child is under the age of eighteen years and not otherwise emancipated.
  3. In this Possession Order "Weekends" are determined by the Friday that begins the weekend. To determine whether a weekend is odd or even look to the Friday of the weekend and determine which Friday of the year it is. (Example the 3rd Friday of the year is an odd weekend, the 42nd Friday of the year is an even weekend).

(b) Mutual Agreement or Specified Terms for Possession

IT IS ORDERED that the conservators shall have possession of the child at times mutually agreed to in advance by the parties, and, in the absence of mutual agreement, it is ORDERED that the conservators shall have possession of the child under the specified terms set out in this Possession Order.

(c) 50/50 Possession Periods

IT IS ORDERED that the following possession provisions shall apply:

<u>MOTHER's Periods of Possession</u>

MOTHER shall have the right to possession of the child as follows:

1. Weekends- Every other weekend, beginning at the time the child's school resumes, or 8:00 a.m. if school is not in session, on every other Friday beginning March 11, 2016, and ending at the time the child's school resumes on Monday after the weekend, or 8:00 a.m. if school is not in session.

2. <u>Mondays and Tuesdays</u> – On Monday and Tuesday of every other week beginning on March 21, 2016, starting at the time the child's school resumes on Monday, or 8:00 a.m. if school is not in session and ending at the time the child's school resumes on the following Wednesday or 8:00 a.m. if school is not in session.

3. <u>Wednesdays and Thursdays</u> - On Wednesday and Thursday of every other week beginning on March 30, 2016, starting at the time the child's school resumes on the following Wednesday or 8:00 a.m. if school is not in session and ending at the time the child's school resumes on the following Friday, or 8:00 a.m. if school is not in session.

4.   Extended Periods of Summer Possession during even numbered years - Upon written notice by April 1 of each even year to FATHER by MOTHER of dates specifying an extended periods of summer possession for that year, MOTHER shall have possession of the child for two periods of seven (7) days beginning no earlier than the day after the children's school is dismissed for the summer vacation and ending no later than seven (7) days prior to school resuming at the end of the summer vacation and beginning on a Friday that MOTHER is scheduled to begin her weekend possession. These periods of possession shall begin and end at 6:00 p.m. These periods shall not conflict with FATHER's Father's day possession.

5.   Extended Periods of Summer Possession during odd numbered years - Upon written notice by April 15 of each odd year to FATHER by MOTHER of dates specifying an extended periods of summer possession for that year, MOTHER shall have possession of the child for two periods of seven (7) days beginning no earlier than the day after the child's school is dismissed for the summer vacation and ending no later than seven (7) days prior to school resuming at the end of the summer vacation, and beginning on a Friday that MOTHER is scheduled to begin her weekend possession. These periods of possession shall begin and end at 8:00 a.m. MOTHER's extended period of summer possession in odd numbered years can not conflict with FATHER's designated extended period of summer possession and with his Father's day possession.

6. Extended Periods of Summer Possession in all years if she fails to give notice - If MOTHER fails to give FATHER notice of her extended summer possession by the dates required then she may give FATHER fourteen days' written notice in which MOTHER may designate dates specifying extended periods of summer possession for that year, MOTHER shall have possession of the child for two periods of seven (7) days beginning no earlier than the day after the child's school is dismissed for the summer vacation and ending no later than seven (7) days prior to school resuming at the end of the summer vacation. These periods of possession shall begin at 8:00 a.m. on a Friday that MOTHER is scheduled to begin her weekend possession and end at 8:00 a.m. the following Friday, provided that the periods so designated do not interfere with FATHER's periods of extended summer possession that he has designated previously and with his Father's day possession.

7. Spring Break in Even-Numbered Years - In even-numbered years, MOTHER, shall have the right to possession of the child beginning at the time school is dismissed for the school›s spring vacation and ending at 6:00 p.m. on the Sunday before school resumes after that vacation.

FATHER's Periods of Possession
FATHER shall have the right to possession of the child as follows

1. Weekends- Every other weekend, beginning at the time the child's school resumes, or 8:00 a.m. if

school is not in session, on every other Friday beginning March 18, 2016, and ending at the time the child's school resumes on Monday after the weekend, or 8:00 a.m. if school is not in session.

2. <u>Mondays and Tuesdays</u> – On Monday and Tuesday of every other week beginning on March 28, 2016, starting at the time the child's school resumes on Monday, or 8:00 a.m. if school is not in session and ending at the time the child's school resumes on the following Wednesday or 8:00 a.m. if school is not in session.

3. <u>Wednesdays and Thursdays</u> - On Wednesday and Thursday of every other week beginning on March 23, 2016, starting at the time the child's school resumes on the following Wednesday or 8:00 a.m. if school is not in session and ending at the time the child's school resumes on the following Friday, or 8:00 a.m. if school is not in session.

4. Extended Periods of Summer Possession during even numbered years. Upon written notice by April 15 of each even year to MOTHER by FATHER of dates specifying an extended periods of summer possession for that year, FATHER shall have possession of the child for two periods of seven (7) days beginning no earlier than the day after the children's school is dismissed for the summer vacation and ending no later than seven (7) days prior to school resuming at the end of the summer vacation and beginning on a Friday that the FATHER is scheduled to begin his weekend possession. These periods of possession shall begin and end at 8:00 a.m. FATHER' extended period of summer posses-

sion in even numbered years can not conflict with MOTHER' designated extended period of summer possession.

5. Extended Periods of Summer Possession during odd numbered years. Upon written notice by April 1 of each odd year to MOTHER by FATHER of dates specifying an extended periods of summer possession for that year, FATHER shall have possession of the child for two periods of seven (7) days beginning no earlier than the day after the child's school is dismissed for the summer vacation and ending no later than seven (7) days prior to school resuming at the end of the summer vacation, and beginning on a Friday that the FATHER is scheduled to begin his weekend possession. These periods of possession shall begin and end at 8:00 a.m.

6. Extended Periods of Summer Possession in all years if he fails to give notice. If FATHER fails to give MOTHER notice of his extended summer possession by the dates required then he may give MOTHER fourteen days' written notice in which FATHER may designate dates specifying extended periods of summer possession for that year, FATHER shall have possession of the child for two periods of seven (7) days beginning no earlier than the day after the child's school is dismissed for the summer vacation and ending no later than seven (7) days prior to school resuming at the end of the summer vacation. These periods of possession shall begin at 8:00 a.m. on a Friday that MOTHER is scheduled to begin her weekend possession and end at 8:00 a.m. the following Friday provided

that the periods so designated do not interfere with MOTHER's periods of extended summer possession she has designated previously.

7. Spring Break in Odd-Numbered Years - In odd-numbered years, FATHER shall have the right to possession of the child beginning at the time school is dismissed for the school's spring vacation and ending at 6:00 p.m. on the Sunday before school resumes after that vacation.

(d) Holidays

Notwithstanding the weekend and weekday periods of possession of the parties, FATHER and MOTHER shall have the right to possession of the child as follows:

1. Christmas Holidays in Odd-Numbered Years - In odd-numbered years, MOTHER shall have the right to possession of the child beginning at 6:00 p.m. on the day the child is dismissed from school for the Christmas school vacation and ending at noon on December 28, and FATHER shall have the right to possession of the child beginning at noon on December 28 and ending at 6:00 p.m. on the day before school resumes after that Christmas school vacation.

2. Christmas Holidays in Even-Numbered Years beginning with 2017 - In even-numbered years beginning with 2017, FATHER shall have the right to possession of the child beginning at 6:00 p.m. on the day the child is dismissed from school for the Christmas school vacation and ending at noon on December 28, and MOTHER shall have the right

to possession of the child beginning at noon on December 28 and ending at 6:00 p.m. on the day before school resumes after that Christmas school vacation.

3. Thanksgiving in Odd-Numbered Years - In odd-numbered years, Larry Allen Lawrence, II shall have the right to possession of the child beginning at 6:00 p.m. Sunday preceding Thanksgiving and ending at 6:00 p.m. on the Sunday following Thanksgiving.

4. Thanksgiving in Even-Numbered Years - In even-numbered years, MOTHER shall have the right to possession of the child beginning at 6:00 p.m. Sunday preceding Thanksgiving and ending at 6:00 p.m. on the Sunday following Thanksgiving.

5. Child›s Birthday - If a parent is not otherwise entitled under this Possession Order to present possession of the child on the child›s birthday, that parent shall have possession of the child and the child's minor sibling beginning at 6:00 p.m. and ending at 8:00 p.m. on that day, provided that that parent picks up the child from the other parent›s residence and returns the child to that same place.

6. Father›s Day Weekend - FATHER shall have the right to possession of the child each year, beginning at 6:00 p.m. on the Friday preceding Father›s Day and ending at 6:00 p.m. on Father›s Day, provided that if FATHER is not otherwise entitled under this Possession Order to present possession of the child, he shall pick up the child from MOTHER's residence and return the child to that same place.

7. Mother›s Day Weekend - MOTHER shall have the

right to possession of the child each year, beginning at 6:00 p.m. on the Friday preceding Mother›s Day and ending at 6:00 p.m. on Mother›s Day, provided that if MOTHER is not otherwise entitled under this Possession Order to present possession of the child, she shall pick up the child from FATHER's residence and return the child to that same place.

(e) General Terms and Conditions

Except as otherwise explicitly provided in this Possession Order, the terms and conditions of possession of the child that apply regardless of the distance between the residence of a parent and the child are as follows:

1. Surrender of Child by FATHER – FATHER is ORDERED to surrender the child to MOTHER at the residence of MOTHER at the end of each period of possession.

    If a period of possession by MOTHER begins at the time the child›s school is regularly dismissed, FATHER is ORDERED to surrender the child to MOTHER at the beginning of each such period of possession at the school in which the child is enrolled. If the child is not in school, FATHER will deliver the child to the residence of MOTHER at 8:00 a.m., and FATHER is ORDERED to surrender the child to MOTHER at the residence of MOTHER at 8:00 a.m. under these circumstances.

2. Surrender of Child by MOTHER - MOTHER is ORDERED to surrender the child to FATHER at the residence of FATHER at the end of each period of possession.

If a period of possession by FATHER begins at the time the child›s school is regularly dismissed, MOTHER is ORDERED to surrender the child to FATHER at the beginning of each such period of possession at the school in which the child is enrolled. If the child is not in school, MOTHER will deliver the child to the residence of FATHER at 8:00 a.m., and MOTHER is ORDERED to surrender the child to FATHER at the residence of FATHER at 8:00 a.m. under these circumstances.

3. Personal Effects - Each conservator is ORDERED to return with the child the personal effects that the child brought at the beginning of the period of possession.

4. Designation of Competent Adult - Each conservator may designate any competent adult to pick up and return the child, as applicable. IT IS ORDERED that a conservator or a designated competent adult be present when the child is picked up or returned.

5. Inability to Exercise Possession - Each conservator is ORDERED to give notice to the person in possession of the child on each occasion that the conservator will be unable to exercise that conservator›s right of possession for any specified period.

6. Written Notice - Written notice, including notice provided by e-mail, or facsimile, shall be deemed to have been timely made if received or, if applicable, postmarked before or at the time that notice is due. Each conservator is ORDERED to notify the other conservator of any change in the conservator›s electronic mail address or facsimile number within twenty-four hours after the change.

7. Notice to School and Other Conservator - If the conservator who is in possession of the child is not going to have the child at school at the time school begins for any reason then the conservator who is in possession of the child shall immediately notify the school/daycare and the other conservator that the child will be late to school/daycare or not attending school/daycare that day.

8. Right of First Refusal – For overnight periods of possession, the parents agree to first offer the child care to the other parent before seeking any other care. Each parent is to notify the other parent within two (2) days of when the child care is anticipated, or if unable to give notice before two (2) days, as soon as known that child care is required. The other parent is not required to provide the case, but has the first option to accept the same.

This concludes the Possession Order.

2. Other Parenting Plan Provisions

In addition to all other provisions for possession provided in this decree, the following periods of possession are ORDERED:

1. Educational Expenses and Choice of School – IT IS ORDERED that FATHER shall pay 100% of the cost of:
   a. Private school tuition at St. Andrews Christian Academy.
   b. All other expenses associated with school activities including: uniforms, class trips,

activity fees, book fees, fees for AP classes, and transportation, as agreed.

IT IS ORDERED and the parties AGREE that the child will continue to attend the Covenant Christian Academy until such time as the parties agree otherwise in writing that the child shall no longer attend this school.

3. Extracurricular Activities –

IT IS ORDERED that MOTHER and FATHER are enjoined from enrolling a child the subject of this suit in more than one extracurricular activity at any one time that will occur during the non-enrolling parent's periods of possession, (extracurricular activities are defined as any activity which is not school sponsored) unless otherwise agreed to in writing by the parties. IT IS FURTHER ORDERED that the enrolling parent must designate each individual extracurricular activity at the beginning of the activity (whether it be the season, class, etc.) IT IS ADDITIONALLY ORDERED that if a parent desires to enroll a child in any additional extracurricular activities that will occur during the non-enrolling parent's periods of possession, the enrolling parent must get the written consent of the other party, if written consent is not obtained then the non-enrolling parent is not obligated to take the child to the additional extracurricular activities. Each parent shall notify the other party when they exercise their right to enroll a child in an extracurricular activity and shall provide the other Party all information about the activity including the following: the coaches' names and contact information, schedules, practices or other information that the party who enrolls the child receives.

IT IS ORDERED that the costs of the extracurricular activities for the child shall be paid 100% by FATHER up to a maximum of $600.00 per year, unless agreed in writing otherwise by the parties. Each party is ORDERED to transport the child to any scheduled activity, including games, practices, rehearsals, and performances relating to such activity, on time and pick them up on time and to have all equipment and uniforms or other paraphernalia necessary for that activity ready. In the event the party entitled to possession of the child cannot take the child to a scheduled event, IT IS ORDERED that the other party be given the opportunity to pick up the child, take the child to the event including games, practices, rehearsals, and performances relating to such activity, and return the child to the party entitled to possession. The Party who is unable to take the child to an extra-curricular activity is ORDERED to notify the party not in possession at least 2 hours prior to the start of an extra-curricular activity. Therefore if the party entitled to possession of the child is unable to take the child to an extra-curricular activity, then the party entitled to possession is ORDERED to surrender the child to the party not entitled to possession at least 1 hour prior to the scheduled extra-curricular activity at the residence of the Party entitled to possession. The party not entitled to possession is ORDERED to return the child to party entitled to possession within 1 hour after the extra-curricular activity has concluded at the residence of the Party entitled to possession. IT IS FURTHER ORDERED that if the child has two activities that occur simultaneously or have overlapping times then the parent who has possession of the child will be entitled to make the decision as which activity the child will attend.

4. Electronic Communication with the Child While with Other Parent- *The child may contact the other parent via electronic media including telephone, electronic mail, instant messaging, videoconferencing or webcam whenever the child wants with the same privacy, respect, and dignity accorded all other forms of access, at a reasonable time and for a reasonable duration subject to the following:*

    a. Each parent shall provide the other parent with the e-mail address and other electronic communication access information of the child.

    b. Each parent shall notify the other parent of any change in the e-mail address or other electronic communication access information no later than 24 hours after the date the change takes effect.

    c. The child may telephone the other parent at all times.

    d. The child may e-mail or contact by electronic means other than telephone the other parent between 8:00 a.m. and 8:00 p.m.

    e. The parent who is with the child shall make the child available by telephone at all times when possible.

    f. If a message is left from the parent who is not with the child, the other parent shall assist the child in returning the call that same day if the call is before 7:00 p.m. and if the call is after 7:00 p.m. by 7:00 p.m. the next day.

    g. Reasonable times to call the child at the other parent's home are between 8:00 a.m. and 8:00 p.m.

    h. Telephone calls and other communication shall not be monitored by the other parent unless either believes in good faith that a child is having a problem, in which case the parent shall advise the other parent that the call or other communication is being monitored.

3. Duration

The periods of possession ordered above apply to the child the subject of this suit while that child is under the age of eighteen years and not otherwise emancipated.

Appendix P
Expanded Weekends Sample Language

IT IS ORDERED that each conservator shall comply with all terms and conditions of this Possession Order. IT IS ORDERED that this Possession Order is effective immediately and applies to all periods of possession occurring on and after the date the Court signs this Possession Order. IT IS, THEREFORE, ORDERED:

In this Possession Order "school" means the primary or secondary school in which the child is enrolled or, if the child is not enrolled in a primary or secondary school, the public school district in which the child primarily resides.

In this Possession Order "child" includes each child, whether one or more, who is a subject of this suit while that child is under the age of eighteen years and not otherwise emancipated.

IT IS ORDERED that the conservators shall have possession of the child at times mutually agreed to in advance by the Parties, and, in the absence of mutual agreement, it is ORDERED that the conservators shall have possession of the child under the specified terms set out in this Possession Order.

IT IS ORDRED that FATHER shall have expanded possession of the children during the regular school year, as follows:

1. Weekends –On weekends that occur during the regular school term, beginning at the time the child's school is regularly dismissed, on the first, third, and

fifth Friday of each month and ending at the time the child's school resumes after the weekend.

2. Weekend Possession Extended by a Holiday –Except as otherwise expressly provided in this Possession Order, if a weekend period of possession by Father begins on a student holiday or a teacher in-service day that falls on a Friday during the regular school term, as determined by the school in which the child is enrolled, that weekend period of possession shall begin at the time the child's school is regularly dismissed on the Thursday immediately preceding the student holiday or teacher in-service day.

   Except as otherwise expressly provided in this Possession Order, if a weekend period of possession by Father ends on or is immediately followed by a student holiday or a teacher in-service day that falls on a Monday during the regular school term, as determined by the school in which the child is enrolled, that weekend period of possession shall end at 6:00 p.m. on that Monday.

3. Thursdays - On Thursday of each week during the regular school term, beginning at the time the child's school is regularly dismissed and ending at the time the child's school resumes on Friday.

4. Spring Vacation in Even-Numbered Years - In even-numbered years, beginning at the time the child's school is dismissed from school for the school's spring vacation and ending at 6:00 p.m. on the day before school resumes after that vacation.

5. Spring Vacation in Odd-Numbered Years - Notwithstanding the Thursday periods of possession during the regular school term and the weekend

periods of possession ORDERED for Father, it is expressly ORDERED that Mother shall have a superior right of possession of the child in odd-numbered years, beginning the time the child is dismissed from school for the school›s spring vacation and ending at 6:00 p.m. on the day before school resumes after that vacation.

6. Christmas Holidays in Even-Numbered Years – Father and Mother shall have the right to possession of the child as follows:

   In even-numbered years, Father shall have the right to possession of the child beginning at the time the child is dismissed from school for the Christmas school vacation and ending at noon on December 28, and Mother shall have the right to possession of the child beginning at noon on December 28 and ending at 6:00 p.m. on the day before school resumes after that Christmas school vacation.

7. Christmas Holidays in Odd-Numbered Years – Father and Mother shall have the right to possession of the child as follows:

   In odd-numbered years, Mother shall have the right to possession of the child beginning at the time the child is dismissed from school for the Christmas school vacation and ending at noon on December 28, and Father shall have the right to possession of the child beginning at noon on December 28 and ending at 6:00 p.m. on the day before school resumes after that Christmas school vacation.

8. Thanksgiving in Odd-Numbered Years – In odd-numbered years, Father shall have the right to possession of the child beginning at the time school

recesses on the day the child is dismissed from school for the Thanksgiving holiday and ending at 6:00 p.m. on the Sunday following Thanksgiving.

9. Thanksgiving in Even-Numbered Years – In even-numbered years, Mother shall have the right to possession of the child beginning at the time school recesses on the day the child is dismissed from school for the Thanksgiving holiday and ending at 6:00 p.m. on the Sunday following Thanksgiving.

10. Child's Birthday – If a parent is not otherwise entitled under this Possession Order to present possession of the child on the child's birthday, that parent shall have possession of all the minor children beginning at 6:00 p.m. and ending at 8:00 p.m. on that day, provided that that parent picks up the child from the other parent's residence and returns the child to that same place.

11. Father's Day – Father shall have the right to possession of the child each year, beginning at 6:00 p.m. on the Friday preceding Father's Day and ending at 6:00 p.m. on Father's Day, provided that if Father is not otherwise entitled under this Possession Order to present possession of the child, he shall pick up the child from Mother's residence and return the child to that same place.

12. Mother's Day – Mother shall have the right to possession of the child each year, beginning at 6:00 p.m. on the Friday preceding Mother's Day and ending at 6:00 p.m. on Mother's Day, provided that if Mother is not otherwise entitled under this Possession Order to present possession of the child, she

shall pick up the child from Father's residence and return the child to that same place.

Possession During the Children's Summer School Vacation

The Court finds that the parties have agreed and it is accordingly ORDERED that the parties shall equally divide possession of the children during the summer school vacation as follows:

Each year, beginning in 2016 and thereafter, the parties will exchange camp schedule information for the upcoming summer vacation from school no later than April 1st of that year. The parties shall agree on the camps the children will attend for that summer.

In the even-numbered years Father shall have exclusive, uninterrupted possession of the children for the first two weeks of August, or such other two-week period he may, at his sole option, select. No camps shall be scheduled during this time without the written consent of Father, via Our Family Wizard. In the even-numbered years, Mother shall designate by April 1st of each year two weeks of uninterrupted possession of the children for herself, other than the first two weeks of August.

In the odd-numbered years Mother shall have exclusive, uninterrupted possession of the children for the first two weeks of August, or such other two week period she may, at her sole option, select. No camps shall be scheduled during this time without the written consent of Mother, via Our Family Wizard. In the odd-numbered years, Father shall designate by April 1st of each year two weeks of uninterrupted possession of the children for himself, other than the first two weeks of August.

Thereafter, the parties shall equally divide all the remaining days of the children's summer school vacation, to be exercised in one-week or other equal increments, with Father selecting the first period in odd-numbered years and Mother selecting the first period in even-numbered years, and then alternating possession in that manner of all children not then attending camp until the time school resumes session.

Undesignated Periods of Possession

MOTHER shall have the right of possession of the child at all other times not specifically designated in this Possession Order for FATHER.

General Terms and Conditions

1. Surrender of Children by Mother - Mother is OR-DERED to surrender the children to Father at the beginning of each period of Father's possession at the residence of Mother.

   If a period of possession by Father begins at the time the children's school is regularly dismissed, Mother is ORDERED to surrender the children to Father at the beginning of each such period of possession at the school in which the children are enrolled. If the children are not in school, Father shall pick up the children at the residence of Mother at the time school would normally dismiss, and Mother is ORDERED to surrender the children to Father at the residence of Mother under these circumstances.

2. Return of Children by Father – Father is OR-DERED to surrender the children to Mother at the residence of Father at the end of each period of pos-

session. If a period of possession by Father ends at the time the children's school is regularly dismissed or begins, Father is ORDERED to surrender the children to Mother at the end of each such period of possession at the school in which the children are enrolled. If the children are not in school, Father shall surrender the children at the residence of Father at the time school would normally begin at the end of his period of possession, and Father is ORDERED to surrender the children to Mother at the residence of Father under these circumstances

3. Surrender of Children by Father - Father is OR-DERED to surrender the children to Mother, if the children are in Father's possession or subject to Father's control, at the beginning of each period of Mother's exclusive periods of possession, at the place designated in this Possession Order.

4. Return of Children by Mother - Mother is OR-DERED to return the children to Father, if Father is entitled to possession of the children, at the end of each of Mother's exclusive periods of possession, at the place designated in this Possession Order.

5. Personal Effects - Each conservator is ORDERED to return with the children the personal effects that the children brought at the beginning of the period of possession.

6. Designation of Competent Adult - Each conservator may designate any competent adult to pick up and return the children, as applicable. IT IS OR-DERED that a conservator or a designated competent adult be present when the children are picked

up or returned, save and except for the provision set forth below.

7. Inability to Exercise Possession - Each conservator is ORDERED to give notice, via Our Family Wizard, to the person in possession of the children on each occasion that the conservator will be unable to exercise that conservator's right of possession for any specified period.

8. Written Notice - Written notice shall be through Our Family Wizard, unless otherwise provided for in the Decree of Divorce and shall be deemed to have been timely made and received upon read receipt acknowledgment through Our Family Wizard or 48 hours after no response has been given by the party in receipt of notice.

9. Each parent shall be responsible for taking the children to school and picking them up from school if school is in session during his or her period of possession.

10. All holiday and vacation periods of possession shall supersede any normal weekend possession periods set aside for Father.

Appendix Q
Parental Rights And Duties Worksheet

Place "X" in Appropriate Column	At all Times	While in possession	Exclusively	Joint	Both
Right to receive from other parent information concerning the health, education and welfare of the child					
Right to confer with other parent before making a decision concerning health, education, and welfare of the child					
Right of access to medical, dental, psychological, and educational records					
Right to consult with any physician, dentist or psychologist					

Place "X" in Appropriate Column	At all Times	While in possession	Exclusively	Joint	Both
Right to consult with school officials concerning the child' welfare, educational status, and school activities					
Right to attend school activities					
Right to be designated on child's records as person to be notified in case of an emergency					
The right to consent to emergency medical, dental and surgical treatment involving immediate danger					
Right to manage the child's estate to the extent created by the parent or the parent's family					
The duty of care, control, protection, and reasonable discipline					

Place "X" in Appropriate Column	At all Times	While in possession	Exclusively	Joint	Both
The duty to support the child, including providing clothing, food, shelter, and medical and dental care not involving invasive procedures					
Right to consent to medical and dental care not involving an invasive procedure					
The right to direct moral and religious training					
The **duty to support** the child by periodic payments					
The right to make decisions concerning the child's **education**					
Right to the services and **earnings** of a child					
Right to consent to **marriage and enlistment in the armed services**					

Place "X" in Appropriate Column	At all Times	While in possession	Exclusively	Joint	Both
Right to consent to medical, dental and surgical treatment involving **invasive procedures**					
Right to consent to **psychiatric and psychological** treatment					
Right to represent the child in legal action					
Right to **receive and disburse support** funds					
Right to act as agent of child re child's estate except when a guardian or attorney ad litem appointed					
Right to establish the **child's primary residence** and legal domicile					

Appendix R
Property Division Working Spreadsheet Sample

Community Estate of Smith	Awarded to Wife	Awarded to Husb.	notes
House equity and debt	$100,000		
W's Car equity and debt	$5,000		Wife awarded asset and debt
H's Car Equity and debt		$5,000	Husband awarded asset and debt
Wife's savings account #3456	$5,000		
Wife's checking account #1234	$2,500		
Husband's savings account #3214		$2,000	
Husband's Checking account #5678		$2,500	
Joint checking account	$20	$20	close and divide 50/50
Personal Property items	$3,000	$1,000	each keep in their possession
Pepsi 401K- Husbands name		$150,000	
Coke 401k- Wife's name	$50,000		
Wife's Home depot credit card	$(3,000)		

Community Estate of Smith	Awarded to Wife	Awarded to Husb.	notes
Husband's Nordstrom credit card		$(2,000)	
Total division	$162,520	$158,520	

Glossary

A

Abandonment - The act of leaving a spouse or child willfully and without intent to return

Abuse - Physical or mental maltreatment, often resulting in mental, emotional, sexual, or physical injury

Acknowledgment - A statement, written or oral, made before a person authorized by law to administer oaths, such as a notary public

Action - A lawsuit or proceeding in a court of law

Adult - A person eighteen years of age or older

Adultery - Voluntary sexual intercourse between a married person and someone other than the person's spouse

Agreement - A verbal or written resolution of disputed issues

Affiant - The legal term for the person who signs an affidavit

Affidavit - A person's written statement of facts signed under oath before a person authorized to administered oath and, as such, carries the penalty of perjury

Alimony - Money paid by one spouse to help support the other spouse, also referred to as spousal support or spousal maintenance

Alternative Dispute Resolution - A procedure for settling a dispute by means other than litigation, such as arbitration or mediation

Annulment - A legal procedure by which a marriage can be declared invalid by a court

Answer - The title of a legal pleading that responds to a petition and that provides the person bringing the suit and the court with a response to allegations in the petition

Arbiter - One with the power to resolve disputes

Arbitration - A method of dispute resolution involving one or more neutral third parties who are usually agreed to by the parties and whose decision is binding

Arbitrator - A neutral person who resolves disputes between parties, especially by means of formal arbitration

B

Best Interest of Child - The standard by which a court determines what arrangements would be to a child's greatest benefit; often used to determine custody and visitation

Binding Arbitration - See **Arbitration**

Board Certified - Recognized by a Board of Legal Specialization as a specialist in a given field of law; to qualify, an attorney must meet certain experience and examination requirements

C

Certificate of Service - A written statement that you mailed papers to a party or person involved in a lawsuit

Custody – Sole and Joint - Refers to the legal arrangements for whom a child will live with and how decisions about the child will be made. Custody has two parts: legal and physical. Legal custody is the decision-making part: physical custody refers to where the child lives on a regular basis. Generally, the parent the child does not live with will be allowed to have regular visits with the child. Parents can make any custodial arrangement that is in the best interest of their children. The standard for custody is "best interest of the child".

Child Custody Evaluation - An evaluation, undertaken by a licensed professional, that includes interviews with and psychological evaluations of parents, culminating in a report to the court that recommends which parent should be the primary caretaker of a child

Child Protective Services - Government agency responsible for investigating allegations of child abuse and neglect, providing family services to the parent or guardian of a child who has been abused or neglected, and administering the foster care program

Child Support - Money paid to the parent who has primary custody of a child to be used for the benefit of the child (i.e. food, clothing, shelter, medical care, etc.)

Child Support Guidelines - Each state has child support guidelines which must be followed in awarding child support. The guidelines are typically a formula. There are only a few circumstances when the court can award child support higher or lower than the guidelines

Collaborative Law - An Alternative Dispute Resolution method in which individuals, their attorneys, and appropriate professionals work together in a good-faith attempt to resolve the issues involved in the divorce

Common Law Marriage - A common law marriage comes about when a man and woman who are free to marry agree to live together as husband and wife without the formal ceremony. To be common law married, both spouses must have intended to be husband and wife. Only certain states recognize common law marriages

Community Estate - The total of the assets and debts making up a married couple's property

Community Property - Property acquired by either and both spouses during the marriage

Conservator - A parent who is responsible of making decisions regarding his or her child

Conservatorship - The legal word in some states that refers to physical custody, legal custody, joint custody or sole custody and possession of the child

Consultation Fee - A charge for an initial meeting or conference with an attorney

Contempt - failure to follow a court order. One side can request that the court determine that the other side is in contempt and punish him or her

Court Ordered Mediation - Mediation ordered by a court before litigation may proceed

Creditor - A person or institution to which money is owed

Cruelty - The intentional and malicious infliction of mental or physical suffering to an individual; abusive or outrageous treatment

D

Debtor - A person or institution who owes money

Decree - The final judgment of a court in a family law case

Default - A party's failure to answer a complaint, motion, or petition

Defendant - The person the case is brought against, also referred to as Respondent in some jurisdictions

Deposition - A form of discovery conducted while a case is pending that permits a party to ask questions of another party or a third-party by the use of oral questions and answers under oath while being recorded by a court reporter

Discovery - A way for getting information from the other side or other people. Examples of discovery are interrogatories (written questions) and depositions (questions which are usually in person and recorded)

Disproportionate Distribution - When the judge awards an unequal share of the marital assets to the divorcing spouses

Dissolution - The legal end of a marriage

Divorce - The legal dissolution of a marriage by a court

Divorce Counseling - Counseling program designed to assist couples with the issues that will arise during and after the divorce process

E

Equitable Distribution - A way to divide marital property, the goal of which is to divide assets among the parties in an equitable (fair) manner

Execute - To sign a legal document, in the legally required manner (e.g., before witnesses or a notary public), thereby making it effective

Expert - A person who, through education or experience, has developed skill or knowledge in a particular subject, so that he or she may form an opinion that will assist the fact-finder

Extended Standard Possession Order - Child possession arrangement where the visiting parent will have the children on the first, third, and fifth weekend of each month from Thursday after school through Monday morning when school starts, and Thursdays overnight

F

Family Violence - An assault or other violent act committed by one member of a household against another; also called domestic violence or domestic abuse

Fault - Divorce granted to one spouse because of some proven wrongful act by the other spouse

Fault, Grounds - The grounds for divorce include Insupportability, Cruelty, Adultery, Conviction of a Felony, Abandonment, Living Apart, and Confinement in a Mental Hospital

Filing - Giving the clerk of Court your legal papers

Final Judgment - The order of the court at the end of a trial or pursuant to a settlement agreement between the parties; also called a Final Decree/Order

G

Geographical Restriction (also know as Relocation Restriction) - Restrictions imposed on where children of a divorce may live, and prevent the primary conservator from moving out of the defined areas with the children

Gross Income - Income before deductions for taxes and social security

H

Hearing - A judicial session, usually open to the public, held for the purpose of deciding issues of fact or of law, sometimes with witnesses testifying

Homestead - Real estate that is a person's primary place of residence

I

IHOP - Informal, Healthy, Opportunity for Peace—process for a fruitful method of avoid a high conflict divorce

Injunction – A judicial order that restrains a person from beginning or continuing an action, threatening or invading the legal rights of another or that compels a person to do or not to do a certain act

Institution - A type of business entity (e.g., Corporation, Partnership, Limited Liability Corporation), organization or other entity other than an individual person

Instrument - A legal term for a document

Interrogatories - A part of the "discovery" phase of a court case in which written questions are sent by one party to the other, which must be answered in writing under oath

Inventory & Appraisement - A detailed and thorough disclosure of all of the assets and liabilities of each party and whether each is characterized as community property or separate property

J

Joint Managing Conservatorship - Where both parents share the responsibility of making decisions regarding their child; also called Joint Custody

Joint Tenancy - A way for two or more people to own property, so that when one owner dies, his or her interest in the property passes automatically to the remaining owner or owners

Judge - A public official appointed or elected to hear and decide legal matters in court

Judgment - A court's decision

Jurisdiction - The authority of the court to hear a case

L

Litigation - The process of carrying on a lawsuit

M

Managing Conservator - The parent who has primary responsibility of making decisions about and on behalf of a child, also referred to as custodial parent

Marital Assets - Assets acquired during the period of the marriage

Marital Property Agreement - An agreement between spouses that spells out how property and debts will be divided

Mediated Settlement Agreement - A final agreement resulting from the successful conclusion of mediation

Mediation - The process in which a neutral person helps people involved in a dispute settle the dispute

Mediator - A neutral person who tries to help disputing parties reach an agreement

Mental Illness - A disorder in thought or mood so substantial that is impairs judgment, behavior, perceptions of reality, or the ability to cope with the ordinary demands of life

Motion - A party's written or oral request that the judge take certain action requested

N

Net Resources - Gross income minus certain deductions such as federal income tax, social security or self-employment taxes and health insurance premiums

No Fault Divorce - The legal dissolution of a marriage by a court where neither party is required to prove wrongdoing by the other party

Non-marital Asset - Assets that are considered the separate property of only one party to a marriage. Generally, these are the assets acquired by a spouse by inheritance or gift

Notary Public - A person who is legally authorized by the state to acknowledges signatures on legal documents

O

Obligee - One to whom an obligation is owed; a promise, creditor, or donor beneficiary

Obligor - One who has undertaken an obligation; a promisor or debtor

Original Petition for Divorce - The document originating a divorce proceeding that includes the grounds for divorce and the action you want the court to take at the conclusion of the proceeding

P

Perjury - The act or an instance of a person's deliberately making material false or misleading statements with under oath

Personal Property - All property other than land and things permanently attached to the land

Personal Service - The process where a sheriff, constable or someone else designated by the court personally delivers copies of papers that have been filed with the court

Petition - The title of the legal pleading that begins a divorce case

Petitioner - A party who presents a petition to a court; the party suing for divorce, also referred to as Petitioner in some jurisdictions

Private Mediation - Mediation entered into voluntarily by the parties, and not as a result of a court order

Pro Se/Proper Person - Representing yourself in court without an attorney.

Prove Up - Consists of testimony in court giving the judge certain facts in the petition, grounds for divorce, outline of agreements and any other request made to the court

R

Real Property - Land and anything growing on, attached to, or erected on it, excluding anything that may be severed without injury to the land

Recording - The process of filing a deed, mortgage or other legal document affecting the title to land

Request for Admissions - In pretrial discovery, a party's written factual statement served on another party who must admit, deny, or object to the substance or the statement

Request for Production of Documents - A party's written request that another party provided specified documents or other tangible things for inspection and copying

Residency Restriction - See **Geographic Restriction**

Respondent - The party against whom a motion or petition is filed

Retainer Fee - A fee that a client pays to a lawyer simply to be available when the client needs legal help during a specified period or on a specified matter

S

Separate Property - Generally, property that a spouse owned before marriage or acquired during marriage by inheritance or by gift from a third party

Service of Process - The formal delivery of a legal notice

Settlement - An agreement ending a dispute or lawsuit

Social Study - A summary of an investigation into a child's home, family environment, and background, usually prepared by a social worker when a child has been removed from his or her home because of abuse or neglect

Sole Managing Conservatorship - A parent characterized as a sole managing conservator has exclusively some rights relating to the child, such as the right to establish the child's primary residence; right to consent to medical, dental, and surgical treatment; right to give and receive periodic payments for child support; the right to make decisions about the kid's education, also referred to as Sole Legal Custodian

Spousal Maintenance - See **Alimony**

Spousal Support - See **Alimony**

Standing - A party's right to make a legal claim or seek judicial enforcement of a duty or right

Subpoenas - A writ commanding a person to appear before a court or other tribunal, subject to a penalty for failing to comply

T

Temporary Orders - A court order issued during the pendency of a suit, before the final order or judgment has been entered

Temporary Orders Hearing - Hearing for the court to decide temporary orders

Temporary Restraining Order - A court order reserving the status quo until a litigant's application for a preliminary or permanent injunction can be heard; may sometimes be granted without notifying the opposing party in advance

Third Party Neutral - A neutral person not party to the lawsuit

V

Visitation - A relative's, usually a parent's, period of access to a child

Visitation Schedule - The schedule outlining when each of the parents will have custody of the children

W

Waiver of Service - A defendant's voluntary submission to the jurisdiction made by signing an acknowledgement of receipt of the petition and stating that he or she waives all further service.

CPSIA information can be obtained at www.ICGtesting.com
Printed in the USA
BVOW01s1930300916

463836BV00001B/2/P